Florence Nightingale

Florence Nightingale

Compassionate Care for People Who Need it Most

WOMEN OF COURAGE

SAM WELLMAN

BARBOUR BOOKS

An Imprint of Barbour Publishing, Inc.

Cover portrait illustration by Keith Robinson, www.keithrobinson.co.uk

Published by Barbour Books, an imprint of Barbour Publishing, Inc., 1810 Barbour Drive, Uhrichsville, Ohio 44683, www.barbourbooks.com

Our mission is to inspire the world with the life-changing message of the Bible.

 Member of the
Evangelical Christian
Publishers Association

Printed in the United States of America.

ONE

August 22, 1827, was both the happiest and the unhappiest day that seven-year-old Florence Nightingale had ever spent at Tapton in Yorkshire, England. The day began in her grandmother's fine house with a breakfast so wonderful that Florence lost her usual reticence.

"There are more cakes and fruit than I have ever seen in my life!" she gushed.

"An accomplishment indeed," agreed one of the many adults at the table, "since the English breakfast is quite the best in the world anyway."

As Florence savored each bite of her meal, the discussion at the table centered on the unusual wedding that was to take place that afternoon.

"Flo will soon have a double-uncle and a double-aunt," quipped another grown-up at the far end of the long dining table, using Florence's nickname. Almost everyone called her Flo. Her sister's name, Parthenope, was usually reduced to the two-syllable "Parthe," which rhymes with Marthy, but sometimes Flo chopped it all the way down to "Pop."

As it happened, the bride, this particular day, was the sister of Flo's father, William, and the groom was the brother of Flo's mother, Fanny. So Flo would indeed have Aunt Mai as an aunt twice over, and Uncle Sam would be her uncle twice over. Any children they had in the future would be Flo's and Parthe's double-cousins.

The uniqueness of the arrangement did not salve Flo's pain. In truth, she was not in favor of this marriage. Aunt

Mai was her favorite aunt. It seemed just days ago that Flo had hidden in a wardrobe, giggling until her sides hurt, as Aunt Mai looked and looked for her. Was Aunt Mai angry? Of course not. She thought it was a delicious joke. Now dour Uncle Sam would deprive Flo of her aunt's attention. Flo brooded as she rode to the church in a carriage with Parthe, Papa, Uncle Sam, and the clergyman. She thought she should have been in the magnificent bride's carriage with Aunt Mai. This momentary separation was only the beginning.

The wedding turned out to be a nightmare for Flo. When Aunt Mai and Uncle Sam were kneeling at the altar, Flo suddenly felt her mother's strong hand on her shoulder, pulling her back into one of the first pews. Goodness! Had she actually kneeled *between* Aunt Mai and Uncle Sam? She couldn't remember doing it. But she must have.

Mama's eyes were wide after the ceremony. "Flo, what could you have been thinking?"

Papa defended her. "The dear child was confused."

Parthe shook her head. "How mortifying."

Several days later, Flo recorded the great event in her journal:

On Wednesday, Aunt Mai was married to Uncle Sam. I, Papa, Uncle Sam, Pop, and Mr. Bagshaw (the clergyman) went first. Mama and Aunt Mai in the bride's carriage. Aunt Julia and Miss Bagshaw came last. When they were married, we were all kneeling on our knees, except Mr. Bagshaw. Papa took Aunt Mai's hand and gave it to Uncle Sam. We all cried, except Uncle Sam, Mr. Bagshaw, and Papa.[1]

There was certainly no need to record her embarrassing attempt to keep the two participants apart! Though only seven years old, Flo already had a history of other night-marish moments. Strange things had haunted her earliest years, frightening her very much. In fact, at times it seemed as though something was *inside* her. She thought she might be "possessed." She couldn't remember where she might have gotten such an insane notion. Certainly no fairy tale or Bible story would have planted an idea like that. She feared being found out and avoided everyone, throwing tantrums if asked to do anything in the presence of others. At times, she had fought to stay in the nursery rather than attend meals.

"But, praise God, I grew out of it. . .somehow," she remembered.

When Flo was young, social etiquette among the upper class in England was complicated, demanding, and troubling. She once called a duchess "your grace," only to be scolded later because she too was of the "gentry." But when she later called a baron by his title, she was reprimanded because a baron is called "Lord." His immediate superior, of course, must indeed be called "Viscount"! And yet the fears—if not the discomfort—had almost gone away. By the age of seven, Flo no longer feared social occasions as much. In fact, she had even begun to appreciate the rigidity of upper-class English manners.

The custom of "calling" was a perfect example. When the Nightingales arrived in a certain town for a short stay, Mama would visit various houses of importance—never before one o'clock in the afternoon, of course—and have the footman leave three calling cards at the door. Her card was for the lady of the house, whereas Mr. Nightingale's two cards were for both the lady and the gentleman. The cards served as an invitation of sorts. The recipient was expected to return a card or perhaps a call. Sometimes the card obtained immediate results, and Mama and her daughters were invited into the drawing room. Even then, the call was to last no more than fifteen minutes, and the conversation was so bland as to broach nothing more important than the weather. Later, by mutual interest, acquaintances could be cautiously expanded. If a friendship developed, the calls would get closer and closer to the supper hour, eventually culminating in an invitation to dine. When others of the Nightingales' social status were leaving town, their footman took cards around to all their acquaintances to formalize the departure.

"Once one learns the rules," rationalized Flo, "one never is at a loss as to what to do."

The social skills exhibited by Mama and Parthe were exemplary. Though only one year older than Flo, Parthe had always laughed easily through dinners and parties and paying visits. Mama did not laugh so gaily as Parthe, but she labored lightly through her social obligations nevertheless. Young Flo endured society, even losing her fear of social-izing, but she did not gain peace of mind. She was restless, though she didn't yet consider that an affliction. As a child educated by governesses, she was impressed that the great poet George Herbert had lived a scant fifteen miles or so from the Nightingales' Embley Park estate, and she was very familiar with Herbert's poem "Pulley":

When God at first made man,
Having a glass of blessings standing by,
"Let us," said He, "pour on all we can:
Let the world's riches, which dispersed lie,
    Contract into a span."
    So strength first made a way;
Then beauty flowed, then wisdom, honor, pleasure:
When almost all was out, God made a stay,
Perceiving that alone of all his treasure
    Rest in the bottom lay.
    "For if I should," said He,
"Bestow this jewel also on my creature,
He would adore my gifts instead of me,
And rest in nature, not the God of nature;
    So both should losers be.
    Yet let him keep the rest,
But keep them with repining restlessness:
Let him be rich and weary, that at least,
If goodness lead him not, yet weariness
    May toss him to my breast."

Herbert's poem rang true for Flo, for she was very restless and she was drawn to God. Her restlessness was not satisfied by simply keeping on the go—unlike Mama, for whom activity was the balm of life. Soon after the wedding, Mama, along with her daughters and servants, left the Nightingales' summer home, Lea Hurst in Derbyshire near Tapton, to journey south to their winter home at Embley Park in Hampshire. Their route from year to year couldn't have been more varied. Even when a broken axle waylaid their enormous carriage one time, the incident just seemed part of Mama's eccentric itinerary. Flo recorded every incident in her journal.

In Staffordshire, they were guests for several days at Betley Hall, where Flo and Parthe had the privilege of socializing with twelve-year-old Miss Caroline, who was so gracious she not only pretended they were sisters, but treated them as equals. The Nightingale sisters were in awe of Caroline's huge doll, with its own canopied bed and wardrobe beside her own bed and wardrobe. On the grounds, Caroline showed them how to shake inedible nuts from the great spreading crown of a horse chestnut. Then Caroline's older brother took them rowing on a lake.

But one day, Caroline revealed that life was not always sunny at Betley Hall. "Georgiana, one of my older sisters, once cut her arm and it became infected...."

"Blood poisoning!" gasped Flo. Sickness had always fascinated her.

"Georgiana hid the fact from mother," continued Caroline. "She didn't want to jeopardize her piano lessons. She loved her music."

"Oh, pray tell what happened next, Miss Caroline," said Flo breathlessly.

"Her arm had to be amputated."

Flo was chilled. The Nightingale girls had seen little of sickness and death. Flo had no memory of Grandpapa Shore's dying when she was two years old. And when Flo finally met the melancholy Georgiana, she knew she would not soon forget the older girl's foolish act. The forlorn image would haunt her. Because of her secrecy, the poor soul had lost the very thing she most wanted.

Next, Mama and the girls were guests at Castle Downton. Here Flo encountered a modern wonder: a bathtub with taps. But when the Nightingales' French maid, Agathe, turned on the faucet, she somehow jammed it and flooded the room with water. After that crisis, Flo broke down one of the beds by jumping on it. It took all of Mama's social skills to smooth over their barbaric entry.

Boultibooke was their next stop. Flo was surprised when Sir Harford Brydges spoke to her as if she were an adult—especially when one of her front teeth came out during the visit.

After Boultibooke, the entourage moved on to the heights of Herefordshire and the ruins of the twelfth-century Goodrich Castle. The old bastion received many visitors, though its stone floors were shot full of thistles. The arched gateway was still intact, as were some of the walls with their loopholes for firing weapons. All around the castle were white wildflowers called traveler's joy. Blackberry vines abounded and once again silly Agathe distinguished herself by eating so much of the sweet, dark fruit that she became sick. Flo wondered how long Mama would tolerate the young French maid's poor judgment. Mama seemed to shrug off the incident, because she was intent on telling her daughters a story. At this very castle, the famous poet William Wordsworth—still very much alive at fifty-seven—had the encounter that became the subject of his poem "We are Seven":

I met a little cottage girl:

She was eight years old, she said;
Her hair was thick with many a curl
That clustered round her head.

The gist of Wordsworth's poem was that the little girl insisted that her brothers and sisters totaled seven, though Wordsworth knew that two were dead and buried:

"But they are dead; those two are dead!
Their spirits are in heaven!"
'Twas throwing words away; for still
The little maid would have her will,
And said, "Nay, we are seven!"

Flo began to wonder if every spot in Britain was like Goodrich Castle, the site of inspiration for some poet or novelist.

The journey continued as Mama led the travelers into Wales to explore Tintern Abbey, another ruin. The girls were shown the mundane aspects, like the hole through which a cook passed meals to the monks and the large prayer room now floored with grass. Wordsworth had been here too, and Mama recited his poem "Tintern Abbey." His verses caught perfectly the impact of its rugged solitude:

Behold these steep and lofty cliffs,
That on a wild secluded scene impress
Thoughts of more deep seclusion; and connect
The landscape with the quiet of the sky.
The day is come when I again repose

Here, under this dark sycamore, and view
These plots of cottage ground, these orchard tuffs.

Flo was struck most of all by verses that said:

And I have felt
A presence that disturbs me with the joy
Of elevated thoughts; a sense sublime
Of something far more deeply interfused,
Whose dwelling is the light of setting suns,
And the round ocean and the living air,
And the blue sky, and in the mind of man:
A motion and a spirit, that impels
All thinking things, all objects of all thought,
And rolls through all things.

Flo had noticed lately that grown-ups seemed reluctant to speak of God. Why did they always allude to God rather than speak His holy names? Outside the church service, God was rarely mentioned. Oh, the poor people in the village were likely to speak directly of God. But the well-to-do, the powerful ladies and gentlemen, rarely spoke like that. It almost seemed a sign of good breeding that one did not mention God. But why was this?

Mama, the girls, and their retinue of servants traveled by carriage on to Monmouth, then by boat on the River Wye to Chepstow. Again they visited a castle, but by now Flo was so bored with ruins that she quickly forgot its name. From there they departed Wales on a steamship that plied the Severn River, taking their huge carriage aboard as well.

At Bristol, they disembarked and had to try seven hotels before they found one suitable. Flo carefully noted the number in her journal. After Bristol, they rolled on to Bath, the fashionable resort.

"With crescent-shaped streets," observed Flo.

Aunt Julia was already in Bath, having gone there directly from the wedding. She was in town to learn how a certain home for elderly women operated. Aunt Julia, sensing that the girls were tired of history and literature, tried to entertain them, amusing them with stories and allowing them to play with a dog. Yet Flo could not quite warm to her. Papa admired Aunt Julia, and Flo's dear cousin Hilary Carter counted Aunt Julia her favorite aunt, emphasizing how hard Julia tried to be "good" and how hard she and the other spinster aunt, Patty, worked to care for Grandpapa and Grandmama Smith. But even Hilary and Papa could not persuade Flo to really love Julia. After all, reasoned Flo, if Aunt Julia really cared for the elderly Smiths in far-off Essex, then why was she always somewhere else?

Flo was even unmoved by Aunt Julia's old sketch of the two Nightingale daughters toddling beside their tall, lanky father on a stroll. Aunt Julia confided to Flo, "You see that your sister, Parthe, clung to your Papa's hand, whereas you— though younger by one year—independently stumped along by yourself!" Aunt Julia loved independence. So did Flo. And yet Flo much preferred Aunt Mai. Perhaps Flo's indifference to Aunt Julia was due to the singular intensity of Aunt Julia's interests, the hawk-eyed earnestness of Aunt Julia's women friends. Or maybe Flo's thinking had been influenced by nasty remarks she had overheard—not from Papa

14

of course—about women with "advanced views." For whatever reason, to seven-year-old Flo, Aunt Julia and her women friends were a humorless, colorless bunch.

After Bath, the girls and their entourage, with Mama directing the travel, trundled across fifty miles of forests and meadows to Embley Park, their winter estate in Hampshire near Romsey.

There Flo soon had a great surprise.

TWO

At breakfast, the one meal that allowed the informality of family and guests strolling into the dining room at varying times, Flo was startled to see an unfamiliar young lady walk to the sideboard with Mama. Parthe watched wide-eyed as the young woman put dainty portions of ham and eggs on her plate. Who was this modestly dressed woman? No servants ate with the family, except—

"This is Miss Christie, girls," announced Mama.

"Good morning, my dears," chirped Miss Christie.

My dears? What familiarity!

"Miss Christie is your new governess," said Mama.

So she *was* a governess. Of all the servants, only the governess dined with the family. How many more changes could Flo live through? She had only recently learned that Agathe had been replaced by another French maid, Clemence. Mama hadn't tolerated Agathe's mishaps after all. And now there was a new governess. That had to be Papa's doing. He had said he was very unhappy with the girls' lack of Latin, even though Flo had learned a smattering from her cousin Henry Nicholson. Inasmuch as the girls were fluent in French, because of the ever-present French maids, they thought their foreign language skills were more than adequate. Apparently, Papa didn't agree.

But by the time 1828 arrived, several months later, Flo adored Miss Sara Christie. Miss Christie made her want to be "good." And by February, while Mama was off visiting, Flo wrote to her enthusiastically:

I do figures, music (both pianoforte & Miss Christie's
new way too), Latin, making maps of Palestine (and
such like about the Bible), & then we walk, & play, &
do my patchwork, & we have such fun.[1]

Flo was enjoying her studies because Miss Christie
knew how to make learning fun. For example, when the
girls studied the Bible, they pored over it so diligently that
Flo felt like she had actually constructed the tabernacle of
Exodus and Leviticus. First came the courtyard. She knew
the dimensions of the north and south sides were one hundred cubits—a cubit being eighteen inches—and the west
and east sides fifty cubits. She put up in her mind a specific number of posts with bronze bases and silver hooks.
These posts supported a curtain of finely twisted linen five
cubits high. On the east side was an entrance twenty cubits
wide, with its curtain embroidered with blue, purple, and
red yarn. Flo learned every aspect of the tabernacle, down
to the last detail of the Most Holy Place, to the very wings
of the two cherubim that sheltered the mercy seat on the
Ark of the Covenant. Oh yes, especially that.

"To think of hammering mighty angels of solid gold!"
she said with wonderment.

When Mama returned to Embley Park to take the girls
on their customary spring visit to London, Flo became very
unsettled. Miss Christie no longer stayed with them but with
her own family in London. Flo resented seeing Miss Christie
only during the day for lessons. The Nightingales were
hosted by the Bonham Carters, so Flo had cousin Hilary for
company—although this time there was no way to exclude

Parthe. The year before, Flo had been frightfully lucky when Hilary came down with the whooping cough. Because Flo had suffered it already and her older sister had not, Parthe was excluded from the company of Flo and Hilary. It had been heavenly. This year, Flo did her best not to let Parthe spoil her pleasure in hearing Tyrolean singers imported by King George IV himself or in seeing the fabulous relics of ancient Egypt in the British Museum.

After London, the family went to Lea Hurst, their summer home in the heights of Derbyshire. During their stay, Aunt Mai took the girls to Grandmama Shore's house in Tapton, then to the original Shore home in Norton. Thus Flo learned that Lea Hurst was not the original family home but came from the estate of Peter Nightingale. Flo's father had been born William Edward Shore but took the name of Nightingale at his uncle Peter's request. In return, as "William Nightingale," he became heir to Uncle Peter's fortune. Flo's father not only received an enormous annual income—many thousands of pounds sterling per year—but he had added to it through his own enterprise.

"On one of Uncle Peter's properties, your father has developed a lead mine," explained Aunt Mai.

The winter back at Embley Park began with a visit from cousin Laura Nicholson. The Nicholsons were also quite wealthy and lived at Waverly Park, less than forty miles northeast of Embley Park. The main winter socializing among the families now revolved around the Nightingales at Embley Park, the Nicholsons at Waverly Park, the Bonham Carters at Fair Oak near Winchester, and the estate of Uncle Sam and Aunt Mai at Combe Hurst in

Surrey. All the relatives were quite wealthy and lived within a half-day's carriage ride of each other.

Flo especially wanted the friendship of cousin Marianne Nicholson. Of all the many cousins, she appeared to be the one destined to cause a great splash someday. She was the great beauty of the extended family, even more beautiful than Flo's mama. The Nightingales' first visitor this winter at Embley Park was Laura, or Lolli, Marianne's younger sister. Although Lolli was a red-haired, snub-nosed delight, she was only five. Flo would have much preferred the company of Lolli's older siblings—if not Marianne, then Henry. But remembering Miss Caroline's gracious hospitality at Betley Hall, Flo was inspired to make every effort to include Lolli. It was common practice to send siblings alone to visit, on the theory they needed a break from each other. Flo couldn't argue with that. Nothing pleased her more than to be apart from Parthe.

"Parthe is so demanding," groused Flo.

Soon Flo was allowed to visit the Carters at Fair Oak. There she indulged her friendship with Hilary. Even Hilary's brother Jack was nice to Flo, which was unusual. An unexpected event of that stay was accompanying Hilary's governess, Miss Johnson, when she visited cottages in the nearby villages. The damp, dimly lit cottages repelled Flo at first. She had gone around with Mama to leave food at cottages before, but she had never gone inside to help the sick. Mama said Aunt Julia did that sort of thing because the villagers could not afford medical care. Flo had never understood what was involved. Now, when Miss Johnson helped a villager with a sick baby, Flo was seized by the importance of helping. And the essence of the act went beyond importance. The help seemed an act of love. Never had Flo felt so radiant.

Flo suddenly realized she was experiencing the Gospel of Jesus Christ as she never had before. Of helping the poor, the Lord had said, *"Verily I say unto you, Inasmuch as ye have done it unto one of the least of these my brethren, ye have done it unto me."*

Flo was by nature meticulous, so she recorded just which medical powder Miss Johnson used for each ailment. She recorded how many grains of the medical powder were needed for patients of differing ages. Never had she felt so useful. She didn't want her visit to Fair Oak to end. Still, the moment Flo returned to Embley Park, she received great news. Mama had to take Parthe to London for dental work. Flo now had Miss Christie all to herself, which meant her schooling could be more rigorous—without Parthe, who resisted difficult, repetitive lessons.

For one of her exercises, Flo perfected her handwriting by compiling moral sayings, such as "Avoid lying; it leads to every other vice,""Conscience is a faithful and prudent monitor," and "Temperance in prosperity indicates wisdom."[2]

And so Flo labored happily through her penmanship. But such copying was laborious, even for Flo, after a while. Finally Miss Christie allowed her to compose letters. Of course, Flo had written letters before, but she had not reflected much on their composition. In no time at all, Miss Christie pronounced her quite a polished correspondent. Flo wrote to everyone. Because the Nightingales moved around so much, often the recipients of her letters were Papa, Mama, and

Parthe! But she also wrote to her grandparents, her many aunts and uncles, and her even more numerous cousins. In January 1829, she wrote to Henry Nicholson:

Mama went to the ball the eleventh of January, came home between five and six o'clock and stayed in bed till after our dinner. She had on a dark green gown, white sleeves, and diamonds.[3]

Flo loved to write. She went beyond letters and began to write stories. Miss Christie encouraged her to record the life of her maid, Clemence. The exercise was a revelation. Clemence's father had been a loyal coachman for King Louis XVI, the French king beheaded in the French Revolution! Flo learned an important lesson from Miss Johnson: Never underestimate people because they appear to occupy a low station. Clemence related some narrow escapes of her own from death, which Flo suspected were mostly imaginary, but which made very lively reading.

"Why not write of your own exciting life?" asked Clemence in French.

"Exciting life" seemed a preposterous exaggeration, but slowly Flo warmed to the notion. To allow Clemence to read it, Flo wrote her "Life of Florence Nightingale" in French. "*La Vie de Florence Rossignol*" was launched January 1829. She was fortunate that there was an exact French word for Nightingale. *Rossignol* appeared to be a good omen. She not only labored on her autobiography, which she took back to her earliest memories at Lea Hurst, but attacked geography and history too. And her journal was sprinkled with Bible

21

quotations like *"The Lord is with thee."* She soon became confident enough to discuss her studies with Papa.

"Good heavens, Flo, how did you know Ethelred II was the half-brother of Edward the Martyr?" Papa gasped one evening at dinner. "They died over eight hundred years ago!"

Papa was a reflective man, who loved to talk about history and politics. And here was his eight-year-old daughter suddenly speaking of such things. He didn't hide his pleasure, which only made Flo work harder on her subjects.

When Flo again joined Parthe in London in the spring, the subjects were lightened by Miss Christie. The two sisters devoted themselves to physical exercise and music. They later left London with heavy hearts, because their cousin Bonham Carter Junior, whom everyone called Bonny, was seriously ill. Shortly after their departure, Flo learned that Hilary's older brother had died. Flo was consoled by the comfort Bonny himself had recently found in the Lord's words in chapter fourteen of the book of John:

> *Let not your heart be troubled: ye believe in God,*
> *believe also in me. In my Father's house are many*
> *mansions: if it were not so, I would have told you. I go*
> *to prepare a place for you.*

At Lea Hurst, Miss Christie tried hard to keep the girls busy so they would not brood over Bonny's death. She devised projects for the girls to earn their own money so they could help the poor. The highlight of their effort was a party for poor village children, complete with food and cakes and gifts. But Flo also visited cottages and began again to record

22

illnesses in her notebook, how they were being treated, and the results. In fact, by this time, Flo was recording in her notebooks nearly everything that happened to her each day. The character of individuals—rich and poor—she also carefully noted. Was her subject cheerful? Merely agreeable? Morose? Tolerant with children? Playful?

When Flo returned to Embley Park for the winter, she discovered that her father had been bestowed the honor of being named High Sheriff for the county of Hampshire. Once a position of enormous power, it was now a symbolic position bestowed for one year. Flo was nevertheless enthralled to see Papa as High Sheriff ride out in ceremonial robes to meet the king's judges, whom he then escorted to Winchester Cathedral before the judges began their trials. Flo was allowed to witness a trial, a very sad case of a farm worker's stealing beans from the owner. For this egregious offense, the worker was "transported" to Australia, with no chance to return for fourteen years! The punishment far exceeded the crime, and Flo thought it was no wonder poor people feared the law. The trial almost soured her experience of snooping about in the cathedral and seeing the ossuaries—small stone coffins containing the bones of ancient kings.

"One is Ethelred!" she gasped at one inscription. "And this one is his half brother Edmund!" she cried out at another.

Other astonishing things happened that winter. Sir Nicholas Tindall came to their estate in a hot air balloon, the first Flo had ever seen. Then Mama took the girls south to enjoy the warm breezes off the English Channel. At Portsmouth, they saw a yacht race and boarded the warship *Victory*, the great flagship of Lord Nelson's British fleet. Only twenty-four years had passed since the British fleet annihilated the combined fleets of France and Spain at the Gulf of Trafalgar—the colossal victory that ended Napoleon's plans to invade England. But Lord Nelson had been struck down by a bullet. Flo felt privileged to see the very spot where he had fallen, indeed the very spot where he had died.

Farther west along the channel, Mama rented a cottage. The girls combed the beach, collecting seashells. The most exciting event was when Mama rode a fat pony onto a mudflat along the beach. The pony sank! Featherlight Mama jumped off and skipped across the mudflat, but it took their coachman, Joseph, with four other men and their horses to pull the poor animal out of the mud. They said that if the animal had struggled, it would have been buried alive. At the cottage, their hired cook said matter-of-factly that the same thing had happened to her once.

Aunt Julia, who was staying with the Nightingales, raised her eyebrow at Flo and whispered, "Now she tells us!"

When they returned to Embley Park, an endless stream of visitors began. Flo's favorite was Aunt Mai, who now proudly doted on a baby girl, Flo's double-cousin, Blanche. To Flo, she was double precious. Also with Aunt Mai was Grandaunt Maria, who read aloud to the girls every evening. Then Hilary Carter came. Not every day was fun for Flo, though, as she recorded November 15, 1829:

> I, obliged to sit still by Miss Christie, till I had the
> spirit of obedience. Carters and Blanche here, not
> allowed to be with them. Mama at Fair Oak ill.
> Myself unhappy, bad eyes, shade and cold.[4]

But Flo's pain shrank to insignificance when Miss Christie had to abruptly return to her family in London. Miss Christie's brother Robert was dying! Flo had not liked Robert when she had met him in London. He had teased her as if she were a toddler and her pride had boiled up. Had she conveyed her dislike to him? Surely she had. Her reaction had seemed so right then. Now it seemed monstrously cruel. She brooded over her wrongdoing. She must be more careful, more deliberate about judging people. Now the brother was going to die. Could she ever make amends? When Mama saw Flo's unhappiness, she packed her off to the Bonham Carters, who had returned to Fair Oak. Along the way, Flo's spirits rose.

"Oh, I get to spend weeks with dear Hilary!" she cried.

THREE

Why aren't you ready for your piano lesson, Hilary?" crackled a nasty voice one day. "Just because precious Cousin Flo is visiting us doesn't mean you can shirk your duty."

Flo looked up from Hilary's desk. Yes, it was her cousin's thirteen-year-old brother, Jack, standing in the doorway. Flo didn't think Jack cared anything at all about duty. He just wanted to antagonize them. Flo silenced Hilary by gently placing her hand on her arm.

"Hilary and I are drafting a letter," explained Flo through clenched teeth.

"To whom?" demanded Jack.

"To my father."

"For what reason?" snapped Jack.

"Pray, respect our privacy, Jack."

"You get more like your imperious sister Parthe every day," snarled Jack.

Flo had to admit that looking at Parthe was almost like looking at herself in the mirror. Both girls were long-faced, sharp-nosed, rosebud-mouthed, tall and willowy—for ten and nine, that is. Parthe also wore colorful satiny dresses, so all-covering that the only exposed skin was her hands and face. About the only physical difference between the two sisters was the color of their long locks. Flo's hair was reddish brown—thick and glossy and wavy. Parthe's was drab and straight as straw.

"Well, are you going to let me read that letter?" growled Jack.

Cousin Jack was a monster. To date, during Flo's visit to Fair Oak, he had broken two play carts, hurt Hilary's hand, made false accusations against the two girls, and struck Flo on the legs with a switch, inflicting much pain. The outrages were all documented in this letter to Papa, carefully dated February 24, 1830. A lawyer could not have done better, Flo was sure. Just to let father know how "good" she had been, Flo added to the letter that to help in the Carters' garden she had organized a little toolhouse with one spade, two rakes, two hoes, and four baskets. No thanks to the monster Jack.

Suddenly, Flo was distracted by a form flitting down the hallway outside Hilary's bedroom. "What are you gawking at?" demanded Jack, swirling around to look.

"It's just the maid, Molly," soothed Flo.

"Do you know her name?" asked Jack in astonishment.

"Molly?" interjected Hilary. "I didn't know her name either."

"Pray, let me finish this letter," said Flo patiently. "Why don't you go on to your piano lesson, Hilary?"

Hilary was much too polite to object. Jack seemed satisfied too, making Hilary go to her lesson. Or perhaps even a beast like Jack realized the impropriety of remaining in Hilary's bedroom. Soon Flo was alone in the bedroom. She was pleased to be alone. Now there was no need to explain to Jack or Hilary how intensely interested she was in the servants. The two wouldn't understand. Oh, Flo wasn't such a foolish girl to think she would be a close friend with any servant other than her governess or her own personal maid. A servant was to be seen as seldom as possible by the betters. A servant never spoke to a better unless the servant was spoken to first. What Flo really liked was making their acquaintance so she could find out how they kept the house so wonderfully in order.

"Organization is everything," Flo had learned.

In any respectable manor the rules of "service" were rigid. The three at the top of the hierarchy—the butler, the house-keeper, and the cook—were military in their demands. Each servant not only had to do his or her duties proficiently, but precisely when required. Timing was essential. Long before the betters arose in the morning, the servants scurried about stoking fireplaces and stoves, then delivering trays of coffee and hot chocolate to their betters' bedroom suites. While the betters rose from bed and dressed, with the help of their ladies' maids and valets, of course, the other servants busily laid out breakfast in the dining area. Then, while the betters chatted and dined, served by the butler and the footmen, the other servants rushed to the bedrooms to clean them, make beds, and empty chamber pots. Custom was so rigid that Molly wore a dress of pale lilac before noon, indicating she was a housemaid. In the afternoon, she wore the black dress of a parlor maid. Also required were an apron and cap of white, but stockings and boots that were black. Except for those directly attending their masters and mistresses, all day long the servants busied themselves, always one step ahead of the betters. Their very regimented service didn't let up until after the final evening meal was served and cleared.

"Fascinating," concluded Flo.

The staff of servants at Fair Oak, the country manor of her uncle Bonham Carter, was very similar to the staff that ran Papa's Embley Park. Including scullery maids, gardeners, stable hands, coachmen, and such, the number probably reached forty—which wasn't too many, reflected Flo, considering that on special occasions Fair Oak slept up to eighty guests! Aunt Mai could accommodate just as many at Combe Hurst. And at the Nicholson's Waverly Abbey estate, the number of guests often exceeded that. After all, Flo's extended family was enormous. If one counted up all the grandmamas and grandpapas, twenty-five or so uncles and aunts, dozens of cousins, and hundreds of servants, Flo's family was quite overwhelming!

"Small wonder we need to be organized," she reflected.

On the other hand, her father's summer estate way up north in Derbyshire—Lea Hurst—was a reprieve from such an army. Nearby relatives were not nearly so numerous and Lea Hurst had a mere fifteen bedrooms. Nearly half the staff was left behind at Embley Park to keep it immaculate for their return. Lea Hurst was a dreamy place, set high above the Derwent River. Mama had never persuaded Flo's father to buy a London residence. So when they went to the city in the spring and fall, as all fashionable people did, they stayed at one of the fine hotels. Of course, the hotel had to be in the West End. All people of prominence knew the West End was the very heart and soul of London—"and all of England," the residents no doubt would have added without hesitation. It was hard to argue with those grand assertions. The West End sprawled from the Houses of Parliament on the Thames River all the way west to Kensington Palace and its spacious gardens. Kensington, the Strand, Hyde Park, Buckingham Palace, Piccadilly, the British Museum, Mayfair, the National

Gallery, Westminster Abbey, Trafalgar Square—all were claimed by the West End. London had been Flo's world every spring and every fall for many years.

"I must sign my letter to Papa," mused Flo, but she hesitated, lost in her thoughts.

What would Papa think of her letter? Would he say, "My! Flo is such a good girl!"? She wanted him to say that. In one letter home she had written that she had become "more good-natured and complying." Did she wish to please Mama most with that or Papa? Flo had come to know more about Papa now that she could discuss history with him. Papa had gone to Cambridge University, where he mastered Italian, Greek, Latin, German, history, philosophy, and other subjects, all of which gave him entrée to quiet, pleasant indulgences. At thirty-six, Papa gave the appearance of a swaying Lombardy poplar, very tall and slender. He rarely sat, preferring to lean—on mantels, on doorframes, on anything vertical. He even had a special desk made with legs so tall he could stand up while working.

Mama too—the former Fanny Smith—was tall and slender. Yet she was not like a tree at all. Mama was a beauty, but a beauty who worked. Her hospitality was gracious, but it was an obsession. In fact, Flo suspected that Mama rather than Papa was the engine that ran the manors. In the house, Papa appeared to care only for his large library and his gun cases. It was Mama—the "milady" of the manors—who examined the grocery lists, inventoried the china, had the sofa recovered in red silk damask, and commanded the ceilings be painted sky blue and the moldings glossy gold. It was Mama who wrote countless letters of condolence, invitations, dismissals, and referrals. She was as energetic as Papa was casual. The two seemed a strange pairing, but some whispered that when Fanny Smith realized William Nightingale's ambition was minimal, she decided to make up for it by socializing the family into prominence. Such a thing was possible, Flo knew. Perhaps it had not yet happened for the Nightingales, but it would. Mama was a force.

And how nice it was to be away from Parthe, Flo realized as she looked at her unsigned letter to Papa. Parthe was so possessive, so demanding. Flo had written her often recently, usually in the spirit of reconciliation: "Pray. . .let us love each other better than we have done. It is the will of God and Mama particularly desires it."[1]

But fickle Parthe would not respond at all, causing Flo to join in battle once again: "Why don't you write? I should think you had plenty of time, and I write you such long letters, and you, but very seldom, write me two or three lines. I shall not write to you, if you don't write for me."[2]

Again Parthe would not respond, but of course Flo continued to write to her anyway.

Flo's delicious reflections were interrupted when Hilary rejoined her in the bedroom. Hilary was so dear to her that she didn't mind at all. Flo signed the letter to Papa at last and put it aside. No one knew better than Flo, who moved about constantly, that her visit with Hilary would soon end, and so she sought to make the most of each day they had together. Flo was resigned if not pleased when she had to return to Embley Park four weeks later.

Papa, perhaps noting she was dispirited, tried to cheer her up. He took her for a long walk in the New Forest. "We must see the hawthorn and blackthorn in bloom," Papa told Flo. "It's an explosion of white!"

Flo and Parthe hiked south with Papa into the vast royal game preserve. Beeches, oaks, and birches were the dominant timber, but on this day the hawthorn and blackthorn were flaunting their late spring blossoms. Flora were always putting on some kind of a show here. The cones of birches might be disintegrating, spewing tiny seeds. Husks on beeches might be breaking open to drop two or three angular nuts. And the fall colors melted even the stoutest of hearts. To make the forest even more wonderful, interspersed among the timber were heaths golden with gorse and purple with heather. Cavorting wild ponies made the heaths magical. Mysterious bogs and ponds appeared here and there. Flo thought New Forest deserved to be called "Ancient." William the Conqueror had set aside the preserve in 1079, so in 1830 his "new forest" was 751 years old! Commoners often sought to penetrate the forest, hunting game and grazing their livestock, so guardians called verderers patrolled the forest. Often while hiking in the forest, the Nightingales saw the sovereign's mounted patrols in their green jackets and caps. Those who violated the laws of the forest were quickly hauled off to the verderer's court in nearby Lyndhurst. Once upon a time, penalties as severe as death could be imposed on intruders, but now only a poacher caught red-handed would be punished severely.

"Farmers are allowed to herd their pigs in to graze the forest floor in October and November," dreamy-eyed Papa told his daughters, "because then the acorns on the ground are green and only pigs can eat green acorns without becoming sick. After the acorns turn brown, the pigs must yield to the deer."

"How eminently practical," mused Flo.

"Isn't it past time to go back to civilization?" grumbled Parthe, gazing in the direction of Embley Park.

Embley Park was an enormous stone mansion, with large, mullioned bay windows and peaked Dutch gables. It gave an impression of loftiness but of earthbound solidity too. But it was not large enough for Flo's mother. She would not be content until five good-sized families—a dozen per family would be a fair average—could be accommodated at Embley Park. That would require a couple of dozen bedrooms and at least one more kitchen! Happiness to her would be a horde of guests at all times. The house seemed always full of wandering nieces and nephews anyway. Rarely was the baby of a guest not being pampered and coddled. Ecstasy to Mama would be a larger mansion and the arrival of dinner guests every evening that would include lords and ladies, with at least a few barons and baronesses. Viscounts would surely follow, yes, then earls, and why not marquesses?

"And even dukes!" Mama once blurted hopefully.

Flo turned ten on May 12, 1830. The very next month—while she was visiting the Nicholsons—King George IV died at sixty-seven. He would be followed by his younger brother, William, who was sixty-four. William was not highly regarded, Flo learned. Although he knew he was next in line to George IV, his life had been spent in seeking pleasure. "But who could blame him?" argued some. His father, George III, had lived to the age of eighty-one, having reigned sixty-seven years! Wasn't there every good reason to expect George IV to reign into his eighties too? Nevertheless, as King William IV began his reign, the privileged classes speculated about his sympathies.

"His Majesty is quite partial to Whig causes," said Papa, who was partial to the Whigs himself.

"With a Whig prime minister in Charles Grey, perhaps reforms in representation will be made," suggested Mama.

"I'm afraid we don't have the necessary votes in Parliament," groaned Papa.

"Perhaps the king himself could create enough new peerages for Whigs," said Flo quietly, "to carry the day."

"Quite right, my dear," agreed Papa.

"While Parliament is in such a benevolent mood, perhaps they could abolish slavery in our colonies," Flo added.

It might seem strange that Flo, at age ten, could engage in such sophisticated conversations. But by now she had experienced many such discussions with her father and had overheard others discourse about the machinations of power. She was curious and her mind was like a sponge. But an education had to involve more than snippets of conversation. Flo had already realized she would never attend the great universities at Oxford or Cambridge, a privilege offered only to young men of her wealthy class. It made her heart ache to know she would be excluded.

Her one-month London stay in the spring of 1830 was with Uncle Octavius Smith, whom she called "Uncle Oc," and his wife, Aunt Jane, at their home on the bank of the Thames River. She played with Cousin Freddy, who adored animals as much as she did. He had two pigeons until one was shot accidentally and the other flew away. After that he consoled himself with his mastiff dog and a very young goat. When the tiny goat butted the great dog away, Flo and Freddy laughed at its audacity. Then the two cousins spent much time rendering an old sheet into a tent. They attached cords to anchor their tent to pegs driven into the lawn. It was Flo's idea to make a standard naming their tent "Brobdingnag," after the far-off land of giants she had read about in Jonathan Swift's *Gulliver's Travels*.

Such was Flo's world, an odd, rich mixture of imaginative children's games, adult discussions of history or politics, and the privilege of guided tours of the city. While they were in London, Uncle Oc took the two cousins around the marvelous pipework of a distillery, then to hear the choir at St. Paul's Cathedral, then to a gallery of Sir Thomas Lawrence's portraits. Not only was the portrait of late King George IV there at the gallery but also the portrait of new King William IV. Flo saw no strength in his face. In contrast, the Russian Czar Nicholas looked very strong, even ominous in his portrait.

Aunt Julia later confirmed it. "Yes, he is a very dangerous man: one who likes to make war. His armies fought Iran, then Turkey, and now he suppresses the Poles. But he is most dangerous because he is very successful at it!"

Aunt Julia had come to escort Flo to Lea Hurst for the summer. But Aunt Julia's route was no more direct than Mama's would have been. First they stopped at Warwick Castle, where Flo pondered a vase brought from Pompeii that was so large it dwarfed even a tall man. In the same vicinity, they stopped at Stratford-on-Avon to marvel not only at the birthplace of Shakespeare, but also his grave. Later on the trip, they visited the niece of one of Aunt Julia's best friends,

Harriet Martineau. Miss Martineau, Aunt Julia told Flo forcefully, was a literary woman who had not yet arrived. But she most certainly would. Before she was through she would be at least as influential as Maria Edgeworth had been. She could write fiction or hard-edged fact. She was all for the rights of women.

Aunt Julia confided to Flo, "But your aunt Patty thinks Miss Martineau 'too positive, too like an uncouth man, to be agreeable, or even to excite much confidence in her opinions.' But I admire Miss Martineau very much."

"Thank you for being so frank with me," responded Flo.

"You have an open mind? Well, then I'll tell you more. Your grandmama says you have the qualities of 'both Martha and Mary, two excellent characters blended.'"

Martha and Mary? What did that mean?

Of course Flo remembered the two sisters of Lazarus in the books of Luke and John. But her opinion of Martha was not favorable. "But how am I like Martha?" she finally asked with a little anger. "Wasn't it Martha the Lord chastised, saying, *'Martha, Martha, thou art careful and troubled about many things: But one thing is needful: and Mary hath chosen that good part, which shall not be taken away from her'*?"

"You are quite right about that. Martha had so busied herself with making her guests comfortable that she momentarily lost sight of what was important. But her desire to make everyone comfortable was not a flaw in itself. It was only poor judgment when it distracted her from listening to the Lord. You must remember, my dear, that when Jesus came to Bethany because He had heard Lazarus was dead, it was Martha who first ran to Him and cried, *'Lord, if thou hadst been here, my brother had not died. But I know, that even now, whatsoever thou wilt ask of God, God will give it thee.'* So you see, it was Martha who first expressed her faith that the Lord could do the impossible. Mary still sat in the house."

"So Martha and Mary both had their good points."

"That was exactly what Grandmama meant when she said you blended the qualities of the two sisters. You are very active like Martha, but you are also very contemplative like Mary."

Ever so slowly, Flo was beginning to like Aunt Julia.

FOUR

Although Flo began to admire Aunt Julia, she was far from idolizing her like Hilary did. Perhaps Flo was put off by Aunt Julia's talk, which reminded her of some very unpleasant realities for women. Genteel women, Flo was sorry to admit, behaved most strangely. She had heard some of the gentlemen at social occasions say women were pure emotion. It was their nature to react emotionally rather than logically. But Aunt Julia insisted it was artificial. Such behavior had been induced only recently by the popular poets—like the late Lord Byron. "Imagination" was preferred over reason. Ladies expressed this "imagination" by being highly emotional—so much so that it came to be expected they would faint over an adverse letter or a mild argument. The more refined the lady, the more she was expected to faint.

"Smelling salts for milady!" was the common cry in the better homes.

A real jolt would send milady to bed.

Flo soon realized that such extreme sensitivity was not the least of her concerns about the plight of women. A child as educated and advantaged as she soon realized it was the male gender that enjoyed opportunities. Mama's attitude was that the girls should be thankful they were born into privilege. Yet, that was not satisfying to Flo—or Aunt Julia. "Are there any members of Parliament who are women?" asked Aunt Julia. "No. Are women allowed to attend the universities? No. Do women vote? No. Are there any women doctors? No. Engineers? No."

"Queen?" parried Flo, just to be difficult.

"There hasn't been a British queen in over one hundred years," reminded Aunt Julia.

"Some are saying," countered Flo, remembering discussions at Embley Park, "that the Duke of Kent's young daughter Alexandrina Victoria could be the next sovereign when her uncle William IV dies."

"Fat chance!" yelped Aunt Julia.

Aunt Julia speculated that the doddering William IV would die too soon and Alexandrina Victoria would be too young to take the throne. Then there would be a scrap for the crown. Probably there would be a king after all. The more Aunt Julia talked and the more Flo thought about her own future, the more convinced Flo became that she lived in the worst time in history for women. A privileged girl could be taught Greek and Latin and logic—as the Wesley sisters had been in the century before—but have no use for it whatever, except to chatter cleverly at the dinner table!

"Maria Edgeworth and Jane Austen—and someday in the future Henrietta Martineau—offer some hope for women," admitted Aunt Julia after exhausting all possibilities.

Yes, Flo knew Jane Austen had enjoyed some measure of independence. The brilliant novelist had lived near Embley Park, about halfway between the Carters' Fair Oak and the Nicholsons' Waverly. At Chawton, Miss Austen had written her last three novels, the greatest perhaps being *Persuasion*. Before Chawton, Jane Austen had grown up in the triangle of Deane, Ashe, and Steventon—even closer to Embley Park. Not twenty miles away from Flo's home, Austen had written three other novels, including the remarkable *Pride and Prejudice*. Usually, Austen's heroine had her judgment clouded by a lack of confidence, even self-contempt. The turning point—which led to the resolution of the story—was her realization of this stumbling block. Only in Austen's later novels, especially *Persuasion,* did she allow a heroine to be self-confident from the start. Yet this liberation came at a cost, because the self-assured heroine impressed most readers of the time as too aloof and cool.

"Never you mind that her self-confidence caused her to be excluded," asserted Aunt Julia hotly.

Still, it hurt to be excluded. "What a mess we women are in," lamented Flo.

Her woe evaporated though when she was reunited in September with Miss Christie at Lea Hurst. Flo's trek from Embley Park to Lea Hurst had taken four months. It seemed the peripatetic Nightingales were never still. As if to prove it, after Flo had been at Lea Hurst only a few weeks, Papa and Mama went south to visit. Aunt Julia remained to run the household. Helping Miss Christie with Flo and Parthe was Mrs. Marsh. Mrs. Marsh had a history of tragedies, the likes of which few could equal. She had lost her husband, then her only daughter, then a niece she adored. Mrs. Marsh had adopted the niece's children and lost them one by one—all five—to tuberculosis! And yet Mrs. Marsh was very kind and cheerful. Did it mean she didn't care?

"Do you not know the Lord said 'be of good cheer' many times?" Mrs. Marsh asked the ever-inquisitive Flo. "Read John 16:33," she advised.

And so Flo read the Lord's words: *"In the world ye shall*

have tribulation: but be of good cheer; I have overcome the world."

Still, Flo discovered that if someone broached the subject of her lost ones, Mrs. Marsh broke into tears. Otherwise, she was buoyed by her faith in the Lord. Nothing pleased Flo more than seeing someone actually live in Christ, truly displaying the joy of the Lord. Flo delighted in seeing someone who was "good." She longed more and more to be that way herself. Miss Christie and Aunt Mai had reinforced her desire.

Flo and Parthe certainly needed the presence of Mrs. Marsh when Miss Christie had her accident. The day began so innocently. They had gone on one of their picnics, intent on collecting a rare wildflower called Grass of Parnassus. Then, out of the blue, a drunken man lurched his donkey into Miss Christie's pony. She was hurled to the ground, writhing in agony. In much pain, Miss Christie was returned to Lea Hurst, but it was after nightfall before a physician finally came to look at her. Even Clemence could not calm Flo and Parthe when they heard Miss Christie screaming. Again and again. Oh no! Was she dying?

Mrs. Marsh finally came to them. "Oh, children, you're so distraught. I was so intent on seeing Miss Christie doctored I forgot you. She is alive and well. Her shoulder was badly dislocated. It took seven people to hold her still while the physician forced her shoulder back in place."

"Pray to God that her shoulder really was dislocated," snapped Flo angrily.

Why did Miss Christie have to suffer so? Why did Mrs. Marsh have to suffer so? Weren't these fair questions, God? Both were the best kind of people. And yet they suffered so much more than other people. Why? Still, Mrs. Marsh remained cheerful and Miss Christie was her old self by the time the Nightingale girls had to head south again. True to form the Nightingales took an indirect route. Flo and Parthe accompanied Miss Christie and some servants to Buckenham in Norfolk to stay with Miss Christie's friend, Miss Emily Taylor. Miss Taylor was an advanced woman "doing good" by running a small school for village children. She financed it by selling her own poetry and other writings. The schoolchildren helped by knitting slippers for sale. Flo was soon knitting slippers herself. Oh, how wonderful she felt when she was useful. For one month, she luxuriated in her goodness.

For the next several months, Flo traveled constantly back and forth from Derbyshire in the north of England to Hampshire in the south—with dozens of stops in between. But the news she received in early 1831 was so upsetting that she threw aside her life story, "La Vie de Florence Rossignol," for good. Her life was ruined. Miss Christie was leaving!

"I am going to be married, Flo," she said, "to a gentleman named Collmann."

And just like that, Miss Christie was gone. It seemed terribly unfair, but could Flo deny Miss Christie a good marriage? Papa now became quite concerned about his daughters' tutoring. Their departing governess had done a fine job of instructing the daughters in arithmetic, art, sewing, music, and numerous concepts from the Bible. Indeed, she had even pushed them further, getting them started in Latin. But she could have taken them only so far.

If they were to master the languages necessary to be cosmopolitan readers as well as cosmopolitan travelers, he—the Cambridge scholar—would have to undertake their instruction personally. Under his tutelage, Flo and Parthe would learn Greek, German, French, Italian, and more Latin! Of course they couldn't "travel" as ignoramuses, so Papa would instruct them also in history and philosophy. He would hire another governess, but only to continue their instruction in sewing, music, and art.

The other great event of 1831 was the birth of a son to Papa's sister Aunt Mai. According to the complicated conditions of Peter Nightingale's estate, if William Nightingale had no son of his own, this boy would inherit everything upon Papa's death. Mama was now forty-three. There was little chance of a son. To her family's credit, Flo noticed no resentment at all toward the baby boy. In fact, he was named William Shore Smith—"William Shore" being Papa's name before he took the name Nightingale. No one was affected more by the baby than Flo.

"My boy Shore," she murmured as she cuddled the infant.

Not only did Flo feel very close to her "boy Shore," but to Aunt Mai too. Although Aunt Mai was thirty-three at this time, she was much more like an older sister to Flo than an aunt. Even more than Aunt Julia, she treated Flo like an equal, discussing things with Flo as her confidante. Aunt Mai was definitely her brother's sister. Like Papa, she was philosophical and probing. She had sensed for a long time the difference between Parthe and Flo. Flo anticipated with dread the life of a woman. She must have something more than domesticity as a goal. But what? Aunt Mai reasoned with Flo over the possibilities. But the possibilities were few indeed.

"Your father is preparing you," concluded Aunt Mai finally, "with a wide background of disciplines. Wait for inspiration."

That preparation included church. From conversations Flo had overheard, she gathered that many in her family had gone to dissenting churches in the past, churches that had tried to break away from the very rigid service offered by the Church of England, often referred to as Anglican. And yet there was a movement among a handful of English elite, especially at Oxford University, to reintroduce Roman Catholic elements into the Church of England, the very elements the Puritans had removed! Mama was pragmatic; she cared little for theology or doctrine. If one wanted to prosper among the privileged of English society, one went to the Church of England.

"It's that simple," she concluded.

Such cynicism did not discourage Flo from study-ing the Bible and attending to her prayers. In early 1832, while Hilary was visiting Embley Park, Flo awaited word of the first child of Mrs. Collmann, her beloved Miss Christie. When the news arrived, she was devastated. Her Miss Christie had died in childbirth! Flo was reeling. She never thought anything could be worse than Miss Christie's screams at Lea Hurst back in 1830. But this was infinitely worse. Dead! Why, God, why? Flo tried to console herself by remembering Mrs. Marsh's faith in the Lord. But it was impossible for her to feel cheerful. This injustice would take a great deal of reflection. Hilary and others consoled her. "The Lord works in mysterious ways," she said. "His ways surpass understanding. Miss Christie is sooner with the Lord." But Flo found herself reflecting bitterly that if Miss Christie had not married, this would never have happened! Everything lost its savor. Games were ruined. Writing cousin Marianne Nicholson in a secret language now appeared childish.

One of the few things that gave her any relief was wearing mourning clothes as a sign of her grief and her love for Miss Christie. Another thing, as simple as it was, was a visit by a dove to the windowsill of her bedroom each morning at exactly eight o'clock. It was as if the dove were saying, "Life must go on." The grounds outside the window were drab this time of year, the trees bare. The sky was cloudy and the air no warmer than fifty degrees.

"Well, I must certainly leave this sweet messenger a crumb or two of bread outside the window on the sill," she said.

Yet Flo remained gloomy.

Hilary, now living in the Carter's new family home at Ditcham near Petersfield, had a baby brother, Hugh. Hugh was Hilary's "baby," just as Shore was Flo's "baby." Hilary wrote Flo that her baby Hugh was very sick. On March 24, 1832, Flo wrote Hilary, "I am very sorry to hear your Baby is still so poorly, but our Baby is much better for he has got two teeth through."[1] When Grandmama Smith came to visit, this time without Aunt Julia, both Parthe and Flo tried to smother their grief over Miss Christie by attending to her needs. They would care for her just like Aunt Julia did.

Caring for Grandmama led Flo to write to Hilary that

she suddenly realized how much she adored Aunt Julia. Surely that would cheer Hilary, who already felt that way about Aunt Julia. But then Flo got the terrible news that little Hugh Carter had died. She consoled Hilary by writing that Hugh was like a little angel now, even being looked after by his big brother Bonny. Yes, even Miss Christie was there to attend him. But this latter consolation brought Flo up short. Wasn't she being a hypocrite comforting Hilary in this way? Why hadn't she been able to console herself with the image of Miss Christie quite happy in heaven? Why couldn't she visualize Miss Christie delighted to see her brother Robert again? And she began to think that her grief for Miss Christie had become an indulgence, her woe actually self-pity. "Well," she asked herself, "do I believe in heavenly bliss or not?" Finally she decided she did. She took out Miss Christie's letters to read them again. Now she must cherish her friend's memory and not use it to wallow in self-pity. Life does go on.

Flo also realized that Aunt Mai, who was now visiting, was worried about baby Shore. "The little dear is a precarious blessing," said Aunt Mai in hushed tones.[2]

But Aunt Mai and the Nightingales soon celebrated Shore's first birthday, followed twelve days later by Flo's twelfth. Flo had been taught a tradition in which the one who had the birthday gave gifts to family and friends. So through the past year she had carefully stockpiled gifts for the occasion: an ivory letter opener, green silk braid, books lined for writing music, a pair of scissors, and two small elegant purses. Perhaps her own gift was Aunt Mai's leaving Shore with the Nightingales when she and daughter Blanche left for Harrogate. Then, when the Nightingales' own nurse fell ill, it was twelve-year-old Flo who was allowed to care for Shore. Flo felt like she was in heaven. Shore so engrossed her that all her letter writing ceased!

"I have no time for such self-indulgences," she told herself, not without pride.

By the spring of 1833, it was clear that Flo's character was very different from her sister Parthe's. Parthe was never happier than when the Nightingales were socializing or "calling." She was perfectly at ease, whereas Flo was restless after a few minutes. But Flo was not an unhappy child. Life was blissful when she cared for the vulnerable. Babies drew Flo like magnets. There was Shore, of course, and his new baby sister, Bertha. But in such a large family, there were others as well. Flo often ended her many letters now with "Kiss all the babies for me." Oh, she dearly loved baby animals too: puppies, kittens, chicks, lambs, kids, even forest piglets called stripets. Of course these animals grew up and had to be cared for too.

"Like my very fat, happy pig, Toby," she said with affection.

Wild birds fascinated her too. At Embley Park, she was most attracted not to the common white-cheeked sparrows but to the nuthatches that scampered all over the cypress in front of her window. After years of watching, Flo had decided both the tree and the nuthatches were quite peculiar. First of all, the tree, though it looked like an evergreen, dropped its needles in the winter just as an oak or a hawthorn dropped its leaves. The nuthatch was eccentric too. Although the tiny, black-headed, needle-beaked, blue-backed, fawn-breasted, stunt-tailed birds scampered all over the tree every hour of the day, as if it were their domicile, Flo could never find a nest.

"Oh, how I would love to see the tiny hatchlings!"

Observing babies of every kind gave her the most tender, most joyous feeling. Was this a reflection of the joy of God in His creatures? Often she reflected on the meaning of her own life. She so wanted now to do good. But how was it all connected? About this time, she found that the poet Felicia Hemans had articulated her feelings almost exactly. And in each letter to Hilary—which Flo usually wrote every Sunday—Flo now included Felicia Hemans's poetry:

> *Where the flower of the orange blows,*
> *And the fireflies glance through the myrtle boughs.*
> *. . . Green islands of glittering seas*
> *Where fragrant forests perfume the breeze,*
> *And strange bright birds on their starry wings*
> *Bear the rich hues of all glorious things.*

Nature seen through the mind of Felicia Hemans agreed exactly with how Flo felt about "all glorious things," the beyond that no eye could see nor any ear could hear. Yes, Flo loved the magical lands Felicia Hemans put to verse. But most of all, Flo wanted confirmation of the connections she felt herself.

Flo knew her Bible well enough to know the source of inspiration. As St. Paul said in 1 Corinthians, *"God hath revealed them unto us by his Spirit: for the Spirit searcheth all things, yea, the deep things of God."* Surely it was the Spirit who moved Felicia Hemans and Flo herself.

Papa was now very involved in Flo's formal education, and Parthe's as well. In the evenings, he read aloud to both daughters. If he read English classics like Shakespeare's *Hamlet* or modern novels like Sir Walter Scott's *Old Mortality*, Parthe was engrossed. Flo's enjoyment was tainted, because she wanted the book in her own two hands to savor the words and reflect on their meanings. On the other hand, if the reading was in Latin or Greek or history, Parthe only pretended to listen as she sketched, a hobby she loved. Although Flo maintained her interest in Papa's more erudite readings, she was still frustrated at not having control over the words herself.

As time went on, Papa more and more gave Flo and Parthe his precious leather-bound books to read for themselves. Parthe considered this "privilege" drudgery, but to Flo it was heavenly. Increasingly, in the evenings, the four Nightingales paired off: Parthe with Mama to discuss social things, Flo with Papa to discuss philosophy and politics. Politics was an exciting subject in England these days, and Papa's Whig party was pushing for reforms. Grandpapa Smith—still alive at seventy-seven—had been a Whig too, but he was a doer rather than a dreamer like Papa. For forty-six years in the House of Commons representing Norwich, William Smith had championed the cause of dissenters and all the oppressed. Although not an Evangelical himself, Grandpapa Smith was a friend and ally of the powerful Evangelical politicians dubbed "the Clapham Sect." Their main champion, William Wilberforce, who had fought slavery and discrimination against Catholics, had died recently, but not before he knew that his bill abolishing slavery in all British dominions was becoming law. The Catholic Emancipation Bill was already law.

All these things Flo discussed with Papa. The Reform Bill they had speculated on so often, which redistributed the seats in Parliament more fairly, had become a reality in 1832. Many tiny boroughs, no more than deceits to give aristocratic landowners—the landed gentry—more votes, were eliminated. Representation of Ireland and Scotland increased as well. The electorate itself was broadened by eliminating restrictive residential and financial requirements. Overall, the reform doubled the number of eligible voters and transferred much political power from the landowning aristocrats to the middle class.

"But nothing for women," commented Flo.

Papa didn't even bother to say, "All in due time, dear child."

FIVE

Men of England—enlightened and otherwise—were not enthusiastic about rights for women. But problems for other groups abounded as well. Children labored in factories disgracefully. The poor in general were neglected. And there was the question of Ireland. Would Britain ever give the pesky Irish home rule? Flo became interested in these conundrums. When she spoke of them to Papa, she felt her life meant something. And though she wished she did not have to go calling with Mama and Parthe so often, thus being always short of time, she had the consolation that Papa was not neglecting her studies. Flo was soon studying Cicero in Latin and translating the Italian of Tasso into French.

Torquato Tasso, the Renaissance giant, was elegant in Italian, French, or English. One couplet could have described Flo:

In young Rinaldo fierce desires he spied,
And noble heart of rest impatient.

Flo also studied English giants like Chaucer, Spenser, Milton, and Shakespeare. Parthe rebelled; she saw no purpose at all for such painful learning. But she did see purpose in all of Mama's interests. Thus, Flo became ever more attached to Papa, Parthe ever more to Mama. The Nightingales kept to their routine of Embley Park in winter, London in the spring, Lea Hurst in the summer, and

London again in the fall. The daughters were sent often to visit aunts and uncles and grandparents. Flo and Parthe continued to be sent separately. Parthe seemed to suffer most from this arrangement, reflected Flo, not because she was devoted to Flo, but because she had no one to boss around! Still, occasionally they were sent off together. Often now it was in the summer to the Isle of Wight, with their governess along to chaperone.

"As well as to continue our quite tedious education," grumbled Parthe.

But most of their time was spent enjoying the sights and pleasures of the resort island. The diamond-shaped island of Wight—its largest dimension twenty-three miles long—was only a couple of miles off the Hampshire coast. The cliffs of Alum Bay flaunted vertical sandstone layers in twelve shades of yellow, red, and brown. The island didn't lack history, with a castle outside Cowes built by wife-slaying Henry VIII. Nor did it lack amenities. Yachting and sunbathing were the chief pursuits of most visitors. Ventnor, a terraced resort village on the south side of the island, was possibly the warmest spot in all of England.

One day in 1834, Parthe shrieked, "Deliverance!"

The two sisters were on the Isle of Wight when they received news that Papa was going to run for Parliament in 1835. Parthe was delighted for many reasons, not the least of which was that Papa's victory would mean an end to her severe lessons! He would have no time to teach them if he was elected. Flo was depressed. She had thrived under Papa's tutelage, even laboring dutifully over Italian verbs. The sisters now bickered more than ever. Parthe was imperious and hypersensitive. Flo was well aware that she herself was often self-righteous and too independent, even indifferent to Parthe. On the other hand, Parthe felt no guilt over their fights, whereas Flo was weighed down with guilt. The Lord in chapter five of Matthew had made it clear to her. One should offer no gifts to the Lord as long as one still squabbled with a brother or sister:

> *But I say unto you, That whosoever is angry with his brother without a cause shall be in danger of the judgment. . . . Therefore if thou bring thy gift to the altar, and there rememberest that thy brother hath ought against thee; leave there thy gift before the altar, and go thy way; first be reconciled to thy brother, and then come and offer thy gift.*

Much of the time now, Flo was introspective. What was her destiny? Just what was it God wanted her to do? Flo formalized her concerns in prayer too: "Oh please, God, tell me what to do." Sometimes, she could stifle her discontent and become involved—like Parthe—in what was expected of clever young girls. After all, if a woman had no object in life other than making a good marriage, shouldn't Flo hone her social skills? Yet she felt her greatest pleasure tending to innocents: a pet squirrel, a pigeon, or best of all, a baby.

"Sweet little dear," Flo would coo.

Her position began to crystallize in 1834. Aunt Jane in London needed help. She was about to have another baby. Son Freddy had fallen and was not well himself. So whom should the Nightingales send to help? Mama bypassed her elder daughter, Parthe, and selected Flo! Flo didn't gloat, because Parthe didn't care, but Flo did battle with pride over being chosen. She really did seem to be growing into another Aunt Julia, whom she now greatly respected. Aunt Julia was universally regarded as good. And more than that, Aunt Julia was a doer. She had a system. Of all the people Flo knew, it was Aunt Julia who visited poor people most often. It was Aunt Julia who knew all the babies. It was Aunt Julia whom the poor people asked Flo about. Yes, it was Aunt Julia who had earned the respect of nearly everyone, family and friends, rich and poor.

"And my greatest friend, Hilary, feels the very same way about Aunt Julia," she reminded herself.

In 1835, the great moment came: Papa ran for Parliament. No one was more excited about his prospects than Mama. At last, her dreamer would show everyone he was ready to scale the political heights. But he was resoundingly defeated! To emphasize even more Papa's lack of political fortune, other Whigs won gloriously that year! Some of the Nightingales, Smiths, and Carters lamented that the times were not right for a William Nightingale. He was too honest to be elected. But care had to be taken where such talk was vented. Not that Mama's father, who had served in Parliament for forty-six years, would object. The poor old fellow died that same year. But Mama and many of the other Smiths were touchy about it. Bonham Carter, Hilary's father, was currently in Parliament too. After his defeat, Papa grew even dreamier and more philosophical. Flo began reading Plato in Greek. The gulfs among the Nightingales widened.

Fanny became more aggressive socially. She would definitely have to accomplish socially what Papa had failed to do politically. Their separate callings intensified. Meanwhile Mama and the others had to complete their mourning for Grandpapa Smith.

"Like everything else among well-bred, respectable people, there is rigorous custom to follow," Mama said.

Men merely wore a black armband, but women had to dress in black, preferably bombazine because that fabric was not shiny. Parents were mourned for one year, grandparents six months. But Grandmama Smith, as the wife of the deceased, was expected to wear her mourning clothes for two years.

"She looks very nice in her widow's weeds," Flo wrote Hilary.[1]

Parthe was sixteen now, very close to coming out. For a while, Mama considered presenting Parthe to the king and his court on the king's birthday in August 1836. She had just the gown in mind for the willowy Parthe. White satin would be covered with *tulle illusion*, or sheer ornamented with tiny pink hyacinths. For herself Mama imagined mouse-colored satin with pink ribbons, or green watered silk with black lace. Finally she decided her consideration was motivated more by a desire to burst out of her mourning than by any real need for Parthe to come out. Parthe needed more refinement, she decided.

"Europe is just the thing to give both girls that last bit of polish," declared Papa.

"I agree—under one condition," said Mama, still stung by Papa's political defeat. Fanny looked Papa squarely in the eye. "My one condition is that while we're gone we have Embley Park renovated, so that we can entertain properly when we return."

"Agreed," said Papa, his voice subdued.

Flo was more unsettled than ever. Why must she go to Europe? She was becoming more like Aunt Julia every day. More and more often, she was the family member called upon to nurse the sick. More and more often, she visited the cottages of the poor near Embley Park in the winter and near Lea Hurst in the summer. She was at long last feeling useful. Nevertheless, the other three Nightingales planned both the renovation of Embley Park and a trip across Europe. As Mama and Parthe finalized their plans to remodel the exterior, completely redecorate the interior, and add six bedrooms plus two new kitchens, Papa busied himself designing a coach.

"Sufficiently commodious to transport us about Europe for eighteen months!" he told a horrified Flo.

Their imminent trip evoked reminiscences of Papa's and Mama's honeymoon in Europe. "Splendid of the duke of Wellington to clean up that dreadful Napoleon mess," one of the pleasure-loving Smiths had commented at their 1818 wedding. "Now respectable people can travel the continent once again." Mama's family was well known for its social whirl. Pensive William Nightingale, close friend at Cambridge University of Fanny's brother Octavius, had gained entry by his social status and his wealth. It was certainly a measure of Papa's wealth that the newly married Nightingales could leave England and not return for three years! By 1819, Mama had been confined in Naples, where she gave birth to a daughter. The baby was named after the Greek name for that Italian city: Parthenope. One year later, Mama had once again been confined, this time in Florence. On May 12, 1820, their second daughter was born. She too received the name of the city of her birth. Neither daughter had any recollection of this "fabled" trip.

"It all seems rather unbelievable," said Flo to Parthe.

But what happened to Flo in February of 1837—before they could leave for the Continent—was even more unbelievable. As always, it was recorded by Flo, the compulsive journalist of thoughts and observations. She had long since abandoned her autobiography, but she still wrote letters by the hundreds, as well as jotting her feelings into journals and diaries—all of which she saved. Moreover, she scribbled down notes on any available scrap of paper. These "scraps" were not discarded either. No other scrap was so terse yet momentous as the one she recorded before the family left for Europe:

On February 7th, 1837, God spoke to me and called me to His service.[2]

Imagine!

Flo herself could scarcely believe it had happened. And yet, why not? Didn't she pray daily, almost hourly? Hadn't she beseeched God ten thousand times for guidance? Much of what she did—especially the endless social calls—was so boring. And much of what she lacked—time to do "good" things—was so frustrating. Was it any wonder she had retreated into a world of prayer? Who but God would listen to her unceasing complaints? Even Hilary, who felt the same way Flo did, tired of Flo's restlessness. So Flo had learned to vent her frustration to God. And then He spoke to her. It was not a dream. It was not a hallucination. Of that she was certain. God did speak.

But, God, she prayed, *You have not told me what I must do.*

She began to realize that was her cross to bear. Just what was it that she was to do? And why the "call" just before she was off to Europe? Was Europe to be her temptation in the desert? The impending trip had become a sore point to Flo anyway. It seemed so frivolous to her as the other three Nightingales planned and planned. Letters were written. Letters of introduction were acquired. Provisions were discussed and debated. What clothing must be packed? What books must be taken? How hard should the girls study while abroad? Which servants would accompany them? On and on went the debate. Papa's coach grew and grew. Soon it was so enormous it would require six stout horses to move it. At that point, Papa turned his plans over to the coach maker.

Then in June of 1837, King William IV died!

"Good heavens!" gasped wide-eyed Mama as she realized the full import. "There will be a coronation and we will miss it!"

There was much talk of the young Alexandrina Victoria. She had just turned eighteen. She was of age. Wise friends were now calling her Victoria to remove the Russian sound to her name. Czar Nicholas was very unpopular. Victoria was old enough to assume the throne, which should have removed all the titillation about a regency. But it hadn't. Victoria's mother, the Duchess of Kent and the daughter of the Duke of Saxe-Coburg-Saalfield, was involved in an intrigue with the powerful Whig politician Sir John Conroy to assume a regency anyway, assuring everyone the tiny princess was far too young and inexperienced to govern. However, the dying king had made it very clear he expected Victoria to succeed him. Finally, Lord Melbourne, the prime minister, facilitated the claim of the princess. Melbourne, a Whig himself, feared the backlash of the English people against the Whig Conroy—and possibly all Whigs—for trying to deny the throne to the young heir.

"From the very beginning, the duchess has tried to intervene," said some sourly. "She even tried to prevent Lord Conyngham from giving the princess the news that the king had died!"

"I must see the queen!" Lord Conyngham had snapped. About the only intrigues left now were the status of the queen's entourage and the identity of her future husband. The Nightingales were kept well apprised of such events, because Papa had become good friends with a neighbor who was none other than Lord Palmerston. Palmerston was Melbourne's foreign secretary, a very powerful position in government. But in the meantime, the Nightingales would see Europe in their monstrous carriage. On September 8, 1837, the four Nightingales and their necessary servants departed Embley Park. From Southampton they sailed the English Channel on the *Monarch*. Flo's restless walk on the deck that night resulted in one of the sailors telling her of his ghastly adventure just four years before. He had been aboard the *Amphitrite*, which carried 103 women convicts and their twelve children. The ship went aground on an offshore bar and the captain refused to let the women and children be put ashore in lifeboats. Could he let loose these dangerous criminals? The surf pounded the ship apart and all on board, except three of the crew, drowned.

"Another example of Britain's inhumanity to women and children," Flo told herself with a shudder.

It was small wonder Flo was anxious to set foot on the soil of France the next morning! From Le Havre, the Nightingales rumbled south across France to the Mediterranean. Flo's French was fluent, but she felt constrained from engaging in much conversation. More often than not, she and Parthe sat on the box-seat on top of the carriage. Parthe sketched madly. Flo wrote just as energetically in her journal. Never was her methodical nature more obvious. She recorded each sight, the date and time of day, even the miles they had traveled since the last sight. She simply had to record these precious moments as fully as she could. She wanted never to forget spotting across the plain, in spite of the fall of night, the rising spires of the cathedral at Chartres. And in her room at the inn there, she watched almost all night as the moon danced above the spires.

The Nightingales' trip across France was three months of interesting people, inns, rivers, cathedrals, even mountains. Everywhere they had prearranged invitations to well-bred, respectable society. Flo now went to fancy balls. These lasted hours and consisted of more than twenty quadrilles, waltzes, galops, and polkas. To Flo's utter amazement, her dance card was usually full. At seventeen, she was a young woman—and apparently attractive to men!

The more Flo partied, the more she hated to leave new

friends. "The worst of traveling," she now wrote, "is that you leave people as soon as you have become intimate with them and often never to see them again."[3]

Finally, Flo saw the Mediterranean as the Nightingales worked their way east along the French coast, eventually into Italy. Not that "Italy" was one political unit. The country was fragmented among several powers, including Austria. Still "Italy" was a definite ideal, displayed in its glory by great artists like Michelangelo and great writers like Dante. Flo was very well versed in the Italian ideal. Liberal thinkers in England—many of whom had visited the Nightingales—often talked of a united Italy as dreamily as they had once welcomed the French Revolution. In Genoa, Papa and Mama had many invitations. The Nightingales themselves held a soiree. Flo was now intoxicated with the social swirl. After she attended an opera, she wrote, "[It was] so beautiful, so affecting, so enchanting; how could one ever wish for anything else if one were always looking at that?"[4] She fought the dizzying pleasure by trying to insert observations of the poor in the journal. But she felt like she was losing her desire to be "good."

"Nevertheless, in Genoa I did visit an institution for the deaf and dumb," she reassured herself.

Florence was special for her. The sight of her birthplace, Villa Colombaia near the Porta Romana, warmed her. In Florence, Flo's pleasures were even more varied and intense. She indulged in lessons in Italian, drawing, perspective, and singing. She visited churches, enjoyed operas, danced at balls, attended functions at the Grandducal Court, and socialized among a large circle of elite acquaintances. In her diary, she wrote about everything as fully as she could. Again she tried to somewhat offset this hedonistic life by observing the less fortunate. She went to a large orphanage run by a man named Guicciardini. Flo, the scholar, was active too, reading the ponderous *History of the Italian Republics* by Sismondi. She became a devotee of the incomparable Michelangelo, who three hundred years before had also supervised the fortifications of Florence in a war. This she regarded as "good." And she revered his painting of the Fates for hours.

It was summer when the Nightingales reached Geneva, Switzerland. The English there were all abuzz about Victoria's coronation in Westminster Abbey on June 28, 1838. There had been no such interest in the coronation of King William IV. Somehow this tiny, pinched-faced princess, who stood so erect yet curtsied so very low and with such dignity, was winning the hearts of everyone. The coronation was a comedy, however. No rehearsal was held, the feeling being that William's coronation in 1830 was fresh enough in all minds. But disaster after disaster struck. When young Victoria entered the abbey in the crimson robes of Parliament trimmed with ermine, she was followed by eight trainbearers. Because they also wore gowns with trains, they stumbled clumsily behind Victoria, frequently yanking her up short.

"Ladies, please," hissed the Mistress of Robes.

At the altar, Victoria took an oath, was anointed with holy oil, then retired to a small side chapel where she replaced the robe with a tunic of gold and silver, trimmed with gold lace and lined in crimson. During the anointing, however, the archbishop of Canterbury had lost his place in the ceremony, leaving out critical passages. So he had Victoria called back from the chapel to finish that part of the ceremony. Eventually, she returned to the abbey bareheaded to sit on the throne, which had been lowered too much even for Victoria and she virtually fell into it. After receiving the dalmatic robe, stiff with golden eagles, she hid her pain as the archbishop crushed a ruby pinkie ring onto her ring finger. Then she received the orb in her left hand, the scepter in her right, and the great crown, all three far too heavy for her. The entire ceremony to crown Queen Victoria took five hours. As put upon as she had been, others looked more foolish. Lord Rolle tripped over his own robe and tumbled down the steps from the throne. Lord Melbourne, who lugged the enormous Sword of State throughout the coronation, appeared to be at death's door!

"And yet when silver trumpets sounded and the archbishop presented our queen east, west, south, and north, the abbey exploded with cheers," said one observer.

Flo met the historian Sismondi in Geneva. Polite to a fault, he offered lectures to anyone who asked. Of course, Flo was quick to ask, scribbling notes at a furious pace. Sismondi's reputation for kindness was so great, he was constantly pestered by beggars. Invariably he handed out his francs until he had none left. While Flo was enjoying Geneva very much, the serenity of the Swiss town was suddenly shattered. One of the Bonapartes—a very real threat to the reign of France's King Louis Philippe—was an exile in Geneva, and now the French had demanded him. Switzerland refused to surrender him. The French army was coming to take him by force!

"We are going to Paris!" announced Papa.

On the road to the north, the great carriage of the Nightingales passed the French troops that were marching on Geneva. Later, the Nightingales learned that Bonaparte had fled to England before the French army arrived. The Nightingales' apartment in Paris was well situated. The streets of Paris were far more cosmopolitan than those of London, with faces, languages, and attire from all over the world. The Nightingales visited many in Paris. However, one impending visit Flo did not relish at all.

SIX

Must we see the Clarkes? fumed Flo to herself.

A widow named Mrs. Clarke lived in a posh apartment on the Rue de Bac with her unmarried forty-year-old daughter, Mary, who was said not to like young ladies! Mrs. Clarke was a Scot but was mistress of an estate at Cold Overton, in the Midlands. Flo was startled by the sight of her unmarried daughter. Mary Clarke was short, with a peculiar Dandie Dinmont hairdo heaped up over her forehead yet cascading all around her face in ringlets. A children's soiree was in progress. No one was moving more rapidly than Mary Clarke. She was a small dynamo. Flo joined the activity with gusto. Mary Clarke, whom everyone called Clarkey, introduced visitors, participated in all the activities, all the while firing witty remarks. Flo had never seen anyone so lively and entertaining as Clarkey. And Clarkey seemed to know personally half the important people in England.

"And everyone in Paris!" marveled Flo.

Although Clarkey was the epitome of what Parthe wanted to be, Flo was in awe of her. Later, the Nightingales received an invitation to visit the Clarkes again. Only then did Flo realize that the spontaneous delight she had shown at the soiree had endeared her to Mary Clarke, who before that moment wanted no more to socialize with an eighteen-year-old than Flo wanted to socialize with a forty-year-old. The second occasion with Clarkey didn't disappoint Flo either. Again, the older woman was totally spontaneous, saying anything that popped into her head, yet witty and completely original. But now Flo saw another side of Clarkey. Her charm was not just good manners; she was utterly sincere. She urged Flo and Parthe to visit any time they liked.

Flo was overwhelmed. "What have I done to deserve the friendship of such a shining light?"

After this, Paris was a dream. In Clarkey's apartment, Flo found herself talking to historians, artists, actors, and intellectuals of every stripe. Clarkey gave them entrée to all the most entertaining shows, the best restaurants, the finest galleries, and the most high-powered literary meetings. Flo could scarcely believe it one evening as she sat listening to Chateaubriand himself reading his memoirs! But if Clarkey had not done any of that, Flo would have enjoyed her like no other person she had ever met. Clarkey was a complete original. And she was liberated! Nothing was denied her because she was a woman. No gentleman excluded her from conversation. In fact, the gentlemen sought her out. Such a thing Flo had never seen before.

"I truly pity you young ladies," said Clarkey. "No liberty awaits you in England. In my youth in England, I decided I would rather be a galley slave than a woman."

Flo was astonished. Clarkey had made this life for herself. Yes, she was moderately well born, but not particularly wealthy. And she had conquered Paris by her own will and wit. She was a real inspiration. What if one had the social skills of Clarkey and the conscience of Aunt Julia? Why, there might be nothing that woman could not accomplish for the "good."

Alas, their time in Paris—and indeed the European trip—finally had to end. The Nightingales returned to

England on April 5, 1839. The renovation of Embley Park, which was to make many additions and to transform the style from Georgian to Elizabethan, was not complete. So the Nightingales settled in at the Carlton Hotel in London with the Nicholsons. At last, Flo and Parthe were coming out. The European experience had prepared them well. Already the two were quite comfortable in bustle and glitter. Mementos of the occasion for Mama were her daughters' locks of hair tied with pretty ribbons. Parthe's grayish-blond hair was fine and straight. Flo's reddish-brown hair was thick and wavy.

"Coming out" had changed little under Queen Victoria. Although the queen had taken up residence in Buckingham Palace, she still used the drawing rooms of St. James Palace. There for the queen's twentieth birthday, nineteen-year-old Flo was presented, along with Parthe and dozens of other young debutantes. Flo wore a white gown from Paris. By the queen's command, the young ladies' necks and shoulders had to be bare. The train of the gown had to be exactly three yards long. With her train folded over her right arm, Flo waited with the others in a long gallery. When her time came, she was ushered into the Presence Chamber. She dropped the train, which was spread out immediately by attendants. Then she walked gracefully but breathlessly to the throne. The queen's very large blue eyes studied her. There was the tiniest smile on the cupid-like lips. An attendant barked out Flo's name. Flo curtsied as low to the floor as she could get. Trembling now, she advanced to kiss the queen's outstretched hand, tiny and ivory.

It's a doll's hand, thought Flo.

Flo backed off and curtsied again. She backed out of the room, all the while facing the queen. Once back in the gallery, she wanted to scream with relief, but of course she couldn't. That was only the beginning of "coming out." The two sisters then danced and flirted through the "season," enduring more than fifty balls and parties and as many breakfasts and dinners. They also now attended—as fashion required—the great horse races at Derby and Ascot, the rowing regattas, and the most important cricket matches. By the end of the season, Florence Nightingale, the lithe young beauty from Hampshire with the calm gray eyes, sunset tresses, and perfectly sweet smile, was well known among the young gentlemen.

"Certainly *all* the proper young gentlemen," clucked Mama.

Meanwhile, the young queen's reputation continued to grow, taking on legendary proportions. Just before Flo's coming out, Lord Melbourne had resigned as prime minister, replaced by the Tory Robert Peel. The young queen did not like Tories. Almost immediately, the new prime minister challenged her by presuming to replace her household staff. The queen refused, devastating Peel with a remark that she hadn't realized Sir Robert's new government was so weak he had to make sure even her household staff were Tories. He returned later with seventy-year-old Lord Wellington, one of England's great national heroes. Still the young queen would not back down. By then the squabble had leaked out and members of Parliament—Tory and Whig alike—rallied behind the queen. Peel was the one who finally backed off, his ears stinging from ridicule of his "Bedchamber Plot." The petty machinations became a nightmare for Peel. Support for his government disintegrated to the point that Lord Melbourne returned to power!

Of course, Flo adored the queen for standing up to Peel. "He assumed he could intimidate Victoria—queen or not—because she is a woman."

Shortly thereafter, Flo saw the queen's growing popularity for herself. At the opera, the audience stood to face the queen's box and cheered. When the London season ended, all proper people retired to their summer estates, as did the Nightingales. Life was leisurely at Lea Hurst after the hectic soiree season. Flo's only real pleasures were visiting the poor in the villages, studying mathematics—which she found very satisfying in its certainty—and having Clarkey visit. Clarkey was her usual peppery self, confiding to Flo that while at her ancestral home in Cold Overton she had kept her tongue "nailed." As a guest of the Nightingales, Clarkey was allowed freedoms that rarely came to Flo. If Clarkey wanted to read a book for hours, curled up on a sofa, only occasionally exploding in admiration or fury, no one even hinted that it was unseemly.

Most of Flo's cousins visited that summer, but not Freddy. He was in Australia, with the exploration party of George Grey. At the end of the summer, Flo was privileged to ride a railroad train, which from then on would make traveling to and from Lea Hurst both pleasant and very fast.

"To think: England now has one thousand miles of railway," she marveled. Ever the meticulous one, she soon deciphered their speed. "We are averaging twenty miles per hour!"

On the train, the Nightingales chatted with old friend Sir

Frederick Stovin, who was now part of the queen's retinue. He told them frankly that the queen was being tutored in politics by the Whig Lord Melbourne. They read the newspaper together and discussed any facet that interested her. Her own father—the Duke of Kent—had died when she was an infant, and now Lord Melbourne was like a father to her; they were that close. Only Lord Melbourne could lose patience with her favorite terrier and openly call him "a frightful little beast." The queen just laughed. Or if Lord Melbourne would slump into a slumber at the end of a long day, the queen couldn't have been more sympathetic. It was impossible not to tell from Sir Frederick's tone that he too adored the queen like a daughter.

Back at Embley Park, they discovered that much work still remained of the remodeling. Flo and everyone else were inundated by Mama's plans for decorating. Little else was discussed. Would fawn-colored walls light up best? How about gold molding? Could sky blue in the ceiling harmonize with yellow-green fabric in the furnishings? Would red flowers in the blue-and-white background of tapestry chairs be enough to tie into the red crimson damask of other articles of furniture? Where best could they put purple silk cushions dotted with gold fleurs-de-lis? Which carpets are best: Wilton or Axminster? Though Flo was not enthralled by such concerns—after all, Parthe was the artist of the two sisters—she did express opinions. To her, the best part of the remodeling was the break in routine. Using her old nursery as the family parlor was wonderfully bizarre. So was sleeping in the attic! And she enjoyed very much recruiting boys in the village for junior servants.

"I ain't sufficiently polite for such a fine house," one boy answered cheekily.[1]

Flo managed to recruit him nevertheless.

When Hilary visited, she carried much grief with her. She had lost not only two brothers but also her father, Bonham Carter, in February 1838. Still, she carried hope of an independent future, much more so than Flo. Hilary seemed to be escaping the futility of the parlor. She took art lessons from a master in London and attended Miss Rachel Martineau's school in Liverpool. That Hilary would be tutored by the sister of Harriet Martineau, a good friend of Aunt Julia's, was no surprise to Flo. Hilary now read the *Examiner* thoroughly once a week for its politics, a hobby she had enjoyed with her late father. And she rode the railway—but in her case, alone!

Because of Papa's interest in politics and the intrigues surrounding the queen, Flo wanted to be as engrossed as Hilary. But her time was rarely her own now. She very much believed in Socrates' axiom: "A life unexamined is not a living life." More and more she felt captive to her family. There was no hope of college for her. Some men studied on their own like she. But they were given time. Her time was frittered away. As Mama became more and more aggressive socially, Flo had less and less time for serious study.

Visitors constantly called, whether the Nightingales were at Lea Hurst, Embley Park, or London. Young ladies were expected to entertain guests, to converse amiably but not very deeply, or to play on the piano a lively tune, but nothing as serious as Beethoven. Entire days were spent showing guests the grounds at Lea Hurst or Embley Park. Entire days were spent sitting with guests in the drawing room, never broaching any subject that might agitate. Doing fancywork while sitting was allowed, but Flo was not inclined to sew or knit. Parthe had an advantage in that respect, for she could lose herself in her sketchbook. Even if a book was discussed in the evenings, it was generally done with a gentleman reading the book aloud. Papa often did this. But even if Flo liked the book being read, she could not savor it.

"I want to see the words, to dwell on them," she fretted.

There were a few odd times—hours, rarely days—between visitors. Then Flo had time of her own. Odd times. Odd times. Flo began to despise those words. And too often the odd times were when she was already exhausted, too exhausted to take on serious study. More and more she longed for time for herself. She wanted to study deeply, with great concentration, things that were important. Politics. History. Religion. But when would she ever find the time? And why would men her own age not talk about anything of substance?

Hilary—in spite of her relative freedom—was disturbed too. "Why is it," she asked Flo, "that men and women have so few conversations of any real substance, unless they are engaged or married? Must all talk be confined to silly flirting or innocuous comments about the weather?"

"I observed that kind of freedom between men and women only in Paris," said Flo. "You should live in Paris with Clarkey for a while."

But Flo really wanted that freedom for herself. And could it have been she was beginning to wonder if she would ever marry? If that was the case, she might never have serious conversations with men other than Papa about things that were important. Still, if a young lady was alert in the Nightingale household, she could touch on a lot of politics.

Thomas Macauley, a brilliant essayist as well as a Whig politician, was a visitor. So was their neighbor Lord Palmerston, a very powerful man in government, even more so now that he had married Lord Melbourne's sister. Married to the niece of Lord Melbourne was the young firebrand Lord Ashley, another visitor to Embley Park. Lord Ashley was destined to become Lord Shaftsbury. He had studied the right and true then put his convictions into action. He was determined to prevent mistreatment of women and children in factories. One way was to limit the amount of time they could be worked in one day. He worked ceaselessly on what he called a Ten-Hours Bill. In her heart, Flo knew he would someday succeed. His cause was so right. But would it ever be possible for her to study as Lord Ashley had and then put her conclusions—no matter how right—into action?

Some of their visitors said doctors were advocating public health programs for the poor in East London. This was particularly interesting to Flo. There was a great need in England to improve the lives of the working poor and the helpless. But perhaps the poor were no longer so hopeless. Or helpless. A coldhearted law passed in 1834 that threw debtors into workhouses had electrified the poor. Only recently the London Working Men's Association had delivered a petition called "The People's Charter" to Parliament with more than one million signatures. Six demands in the petition included voting rights for commoners, secret balloting, and annual elections. When Parliament spurned them, referring to their movement as "Chartism," the workers struck in the fall of 1839. Many strikers had since been jailed.

"A vote for common riffraff? Never!" said even the most liberal Whig politicians.

Both Aunt Julia and Hilary passed Harriet Martineau's thoughts on to Flo: "Those who have not looked into Chartism think that it means a revolution. But they should look deeper, go out upon the moors by torchlight, talk with an exhausted mother under the hedge or beside the loom, listen to poor wretches outside the union workhouse or workers in the Durham coal pits. These people are suffering."[2]

Then a young writer in London shocked everyone with his monthly installments of a story called *Oliver Twist*. He had begun making a reputation as a writer of humor, but *Oliver Twist* was not humorous. Oliver was "a parish child—the orphan of a workhouse—the humble, half-starved drudge—to be cuffed and buffeted through the world—despised by all, and pitied by none." *Oliver Twist* portrayed the poor of London as no well-to-do person could know. One villain, named Bill Sykes, was chilling. Some doubted the veracity of the story's setting. "Just walk the streets of London if you doubt me," countered the young writer Charles Dickens.

Thomas Carlyle was read by Flo now too. A Scot of about forty-five, he had long lived in the Chelsea area of London and was very popular among the literary set. He was great friends with John Stuart Mill and Ralph Waldo Emerson. Carlyle's opinions were a peculiar mix, but often strikingly original. For example, he had recently championed the idea that mankind was advanced by heroes. The hero was one who was able to perceive the intent of God. The greatest hero was Christ. Flo liked this theory very much. It seemed true. Yet Carlyle had a flaw in Flo's view.

"He tries to persuade by exhortation as if he is some kind of modern-day prophet," she observed. "He does not prove his arguments with patient reason."

Flo, who was well read in English, French, Italian, German, Latin, and Greek, now read novels too. The English novel was changing. Dickens was just one example of the new novelist. The best novelist of the previous generation had been Jane Austen. But she had triumphed within the bounds of manners. Her characters, especially the women, had not broken out of those bounds. Now Flo read *Gabriel* by George Sand in French. It was an ingenious story that showed the predicament of women. A girl was brought up to believe herself, and to be considered by others, a boy, so she would inherit a dukedom. But she discovered her true gender. Then she fell in love with a young man. Eventually she had to choose between the freedom she would have as a young "man" and the love she felt as a woman for the young man. But that story was mild compared to most of Sand's works. George Sand was the pen name for a woman who was shocking even Paris society. She not only lived in sin but also wrote about it. Clarkey would not receive Sand in her apartment, but she devoured her novels.

Flo was very troubled by Sand's ideas. "But I am impressed that a woman could take so bold a stand."

Christmas of 1839 should have been joyous, with Embley Park just remodeled and hosting the Nicholsons and the Carters. But the news that Freddy Smith had died in Australia threw everyone into gloom. After Christmas, Flo left Embley Park to stay with Aunt Mai in Combe Hurst. She was as open with Aunt Mai as with Hilary. What could she pursue to make herself worthy? Aunt Mai was in complete sympathy. Together the two discussed what she might study—as Hilary studied art—and where. In March 1840, Aunt Mai wrote Mama:

> *Hard work is necessary to give zest to life in a character like hers, where there is great power of mind and a more than common inclination to apply. So I write you if you in any way object to a mathematical master.*[3]

Mama did object. How would Flo find the time? And what use is mathematics to a young lady desiring marriage? "I don't think they have any idea of half that is in you," commiserated Aunt Mai to Flo. Aunt Mai persisted, but Mama opposed the idea and raised objection after objection. Where would they find a master who could be trusted with a young lady? Even Papa entered the dispute. "Why mathematics? Why not history or philosophy?" Slowly Mama and Papa strangled Flo's attempt to pursue mathematics. She was more depressed than ever.

But one thing still cheered her: helping out. Aunt Jane, still grieving over Freddy, was expecting a baby. Flo was pleased when opinion prevailed among the aunts that she should be the one to stay with Aunt Jane on the Thames in London. Soon Flo was writing Grandmama Shore:

I have been staying with Mrs. Octavius Smith for
the last week, and have had so much to do with the
children, in consequence of her delicate state. . . . Aunt
Jane is again confined to her bed with the excitement
produced by William Nicholson's sudden departure to
join his regiment in Australia. . . . This harrowed up
old associations in Aunt Jane's mind connected with the
poor fellow who was lost, and has much weakened her.
She requires a great deal of care. The two youngest are
nice little girls and are very much with me. . . . I must
wish you good night, for it is late and I have not much
time to write in the day as I have the children here
always with me, Aunt Jane requiring the utmost quiet.
With best love. . .ever your truly obliged and affection-
ate grandchild.[4]

At this time, all London was buzzing about Queen
Victoria's wedding. She was marrying her first cousin Prince
Albert of Saxe-Coburg-Gotha. Albert was the nephew of
Victoria's mother. By custom, the queen proposed marriage,
and everyone agreed that the dashing, honorable Albert—
born the same year as Victoria—was a superb choice.
Typical of her fiery nature, and against Lord Melbourne's
advice, she invited only three Tories to the wedding. After
fidgeting some time in the chapel at St. James, the queen—
in her great white wedding gown—bolted down the steps
to embrace Albert when his carriage arrived. All England
was privy to the fact that Victoria loved Albert very much.

As spring of 1840 arrived, Grandmama Smith died at
eighty-one, freeing Aunt Julia at long last. Now forty-one,

Aunt Julia threw her liberated energies into the Anti-Slavery Convention to be held in London that summer. Flo was frightened to think her own future might repeat Aunt Julia's past. Would Flo, too, be forty or older before she was free of the responsibility of aging parents? Often now she brooded over her "call." It had been three years since God called her to His service.

"Why am I still in the dark?" she wondered. She remembered guiltily how much she enjoyed the social life in Europe. "Have I somehow defied His will?"

SEVEN

Flo was troubled, though occasionally she still found pleasure in social life, especially at the Nicholsons.' She had little contact with Aunt Anne, but she was very fond of her cousins Marianne, Henry, and Lolli. Their great house, Waverly, gave its name to a series of novels by Sir Walter Scott. Of all the relatives, their fun was the most intricately planned. The highlight at Waverly was invariably an elaborate theatrical production. However, on this occasion they had dawdled too long, considering first this play and then that play. Once they decided on Shakespeare's *Merchant of Venice*, they realized they had only two weeks before their promised performance.

"Flo must be the stage manager," insisted Henry, now a student at Cambridge.

"But why me?" she protested.

"Because you're the only one who can pull it all together."

No one disagreed with Henry. Perhaps Mama and Parthe didn't recognize Flo's steely resolve, but clearly many of the aunts, uncles, and cousins did. Once rehearsal started, the participants were serious indeed. Henry rushed into London to watch the legendary William Macready play Shylock. Flo reigned with an iron hand. She had two recalcitrant players, a naval captain who played Antonio, and Uncle Adams, Mama's brother, who played the duke. One was flippant, the other lazy. In their scene together, Flo was stretched to her limit.

"If you will be so kind, captain," purred Flo. "You must say 'Ready, so please your grace,' not 'Ready to ease your disgrace'!" Seconds later, she was snapping, "Really, Uncle Adams, you must learn your lines!"

Uncle Adams was amazed that Flo was so tough. He responded, even if the captain did not. The play went on as scheduled, and everyone agreed that it went well. Aunt Anne and Marianne were deemed the most successful in their parts. Parthe's stage scenery, especially of the Grand Canal with gondolas, was applauded. After the play, the Nicholsons and their guests danced until five in the morning. Eighty were staying at Waverly. It was this intensity of activity and conviviality that Mama desired more than anything.

"Aunt Julia is too sick to be here," Mama informed Flo, "because she is worn out from her long years of restlessness. Let that be a warning to you."

In the summer of 1841, the Carters borrowed Papa's enormous coach to tour France. Once there, Hilary did exactly what Flo had advised. She remained with Clarkey and studied art. She salved Flo's envy by sending her sketches. Meanwhile Mama worked feverishly to attract guests to Embley Park. She could sleep five large families now and intended to do just that at all times. She was beginning to get worried. Flo was twenty-one, Parthe twenty-two. She was not impressed that she herself had been quite happy to wait for marriage until the age of thirty!

One day, at Lord Palmerston's Broadlands estate, Mama thought she had hit paydirt for Flo. There Flo met Richard Monckton Milnes, an eminently eligible bachelor of thirty-three. Someday he would become Lord Houghton. He claimed to have political ambition, though few believed him. Somehow he had become the center of an elite literary circle in London. Though he had no great talent himself, he drew to "breakfast" at his residence in Pall Mall the likes of Alfred Tennyson, Thomas Carlyle, Robert Peel, William Thackeray, and Alexis de Tocqueville. His chief attraction resembled Clarkey's. He was said to be always amiable, with crackling wit. But unlike Clarkey, Milnes was destined for great money, as heir to an enormous estate, Fryston in Yorkshire. Flo's first impression of him was one of disappointment. He was small and bland.

Where is the wit? What can people see in this man? Flo wondered.

Yet, Mama was not going to miss an opportunity. She invited Milnes to Embley Park and he accepted. There he came alive. He captivated Flo. He was a wonderful raconteur, telling one story after another. Everyone wanted to listen. Typical of his stories was one about a Capuchin friar named Father Matthew, who came to one of Milnes's breakfasts. One of the other guests praised Father Matthew tongue-in-cheek for his temperance movement in Ireland. In response, the friar presented him with a medal. The alarmed recipient later presented the medal to another member of Parliament who was too drunk to refuse it. Milnes also talked about his visit with the notorious George Sand in Paris, cavalierly defending her. Flo had to admit that Milnes was very entertaining and broadminded.

"And he was uncommonly interested in you!" said a glowing Mama to Flo.

The next great event socially for the Nightingales was

an invitation to meet the Duke of Sussex at the Chatsworth estate of the Duke of Devonshire. The queen's sixty-nine-year-old "Uncle Augustus"—the Duke of Sussex—was highly eccentric. He had worn a black skullcap at her wedding and sobbed uncontrollably through the entire ceremony. The Nightingales spent three busy days at Chatsworth. Entertainment was planned for every moment. Chatsworth had not only a great palace but also immense grounds with elaborate gardens and a renowned glass conservatory. In the conservatory flourished tropical plants, a novel accomplishment at the time.

Mama was ecstatic. Chatsworth was the Nightingales' most important recognition yet by royalty. But after Mama's Chatsworth triumph, Flo was much happier staying with Grandmama Shore and eleven-year-old Shore in Tapton, simply because she was allowed to care for them. Nothing gave her greater peace of mind. And she knew many local villagers. Often they needed care. Among them was Helen Richardson. Helen's sister, Hope, had died in childbirth. Helen was determined to raise the baby herself, although she was almost paralyzed with grief. Flo was expected back in Embley Park, but surely Mama would give her time to help Helen. So Flo appealed to her:

My dearest. I write to you to bespeak your intercession, which I know you will give, without my asking it, tho' I do not deserve it, because you never think of your own solitude. Helen is sitting opposite to me to make me say that she dares "not look you in the face it is not to leave her alone now." I sh'd be missing the only

opport'y I ever had of doing real good. . . . My dear, I
cry unto you, do this thing for me for no one else can do
it. You will have me all your life, for I shall never die
& never marry.[1]

But Mama refused, perhaps jolted by Flo's stunning assertion that she would never marry. Flo went back to the social whirl, but something new developed. She found herself daydreaming constantly of doing "good." Much was vanity, she realized, because in her dreams she was admired by all. This offspring of pride bothered her. And were such daydreams healthy? Perhaps even sinful? What was she going to do?

In 1842, the Prussian ambassador to Queen Victoria visited Embley Park with his English wife. Christian Bunsen was far more than a diplomat. He was a scholar of renown, master of subjects as diverse as Egyptology and philosophy. Flo was as fascinated as Papa by Bunsen's discussion of the German philosophers Schleiermacher and Schopenhauer. Bunsen easily discussed theological developments in England. The Broad Church movement was attracting those not adhering to either the Low Church, the Evangelicals who believed truth was revealed by the Bible and personal experience, or the High Church, the quasi-Catholics who believed truth was revealed by the Bible and church traditions. The Broad Church had no unified theology but challenged the Bible and allowed all free inquiry. This very liberal outlook did not shock any of the Nightingales. They were Unitarians in background and had heard unorthodox opinions discussed all their lives.

Flo trusted Bunsen enough to ask him privately, "What can an individual do toward lifting the load of suffering from the helpless and the miserable?"[2]

The startled Bunsen recommended the good works being done at the Institute of Kaiserswerth in Germany. There Pastor Fliedner trained Protestant women—they were called deaconesses—to be nurses.

But Flo was sure Bunsen didn't believe she was really serious about doing good works. So few people were. Besides, how could she free herself? On went her frustrating life. Yes, she was every bit as restless as Aunt Julia. Sometimes she accepted her restlessness, remembering fondly dear old George Herbert's poem "Pulley." Lack of rest was God's way of pulling the weary heart back to Him. Yet, other times Flo became very angry that she did not know how to satisfy her restlessness.

That next winter, she was down for a time with a chest ailment—not at Embley Park, but Waverly. While bed-ridden, she read Harriet Martineau's "Thoughts in a Sick Room." She found much to agree with. In illness one did realize how an instant of good swallowed up long hours of pain, just as Martineau asserted. How wonderful. What could be more beneficial than doing that kind of good for the suffering? While recovering, she began a friendship with Aunt Hannah, the sister-in-law of Aunt Anne. Aunt Hannah was a mystic, who impressed Flo as being more in touch with the unseen than the seen. Flo thought she was the holiest person she had ever met. After she returned to Embley Park, she corresponded with her new icon:

It seems easy to carry one's own Misfortunes in one's pocket, but when one sees dark ways opening before those one loves there is nothing for it but to lay one's soul in God's bosom. Oh, if one did but think one was getting nearer to the Divine patience, when to us as to Him a thousand years will appear but as a day, even as now, alas! a moment of discouragement seems a thousand years.[3]

Flo read books Aunt Hannah recommended, especially those that enlarged on dispensation. These speculated on stages of God's revelations about His plan for mankind. Flo wanted very much to experience a revelation herself, and just as much she wanted to be part of His plan. She rarely forgot her "call," and the mystery that she did not know how to fulfill the call. Yet she was drawn more and more to the plight of the suffering.

Others were concerned too. Unlike Flo, they were actively researching misery and issuing reports. Flo had no problem acquiring the reports. Finding the time to read them was the problem, but read them she did—even at the expense of her sleep. She digested the *Report of Select Committee on the Health of Towns*, the *Report on Sanitary Condition of Labouring Classes*, and the *Second Report of the Children's Employment Commission*. She found all these concerns compelling. And she was definitely drawn to helping the sick. The summer Flo turned twenty-four, Embley Park was visited by two Unitarians from America, Dr. Howe and his wife, Julia Ward Howe. The first evening, the doctor talked about his institute for the deaf and blind. His greatest challenge was to educate them. But he had other concerns. He wanted to treat the sick and the feebleminded. He also fervently wanted to help prisoners and slaves. Flo could scarcely sleep that night.

Next morning, she drew the doctor aside. "Dr. Howe, do you think it would be unsuitable and unbecoming for a young Englishwoman to devote herself to works of charity in hospitals and elsewhere, as Catholic sisters do? Do you think it would be a dreadful thing?"[4]

"My dear Miss Florence," he said soothingly, "it would be unusual, and in England whatever is unusual is apt to be thought unsuitable; but I say to you, go forward if you have a vocation for that way of life; act up to your inspiration, and you will find that there is never anything unbecoming or unladylike in doing your duty for the good of others. Choose, go on with it wherever it may lead you, and God be with you."[5]

Flo felt like soaring to the heights. "Yes," said the doctor. "Do it." In truth, Flo was only at peace now when she was helping the destitute in the nearby villages. In the village of Wellow near Embley Park, Flo offered her services to the new vicar, Mr. Empson. She knew he was trying to start a school for the poor village children. When Mr. Empson and his wife had Flo for lunch, she had to write Hilary:

> *Such a luncheon, neat but not gaudy, elegant but not expensive. Then we grew rhapsodical, philosophical, and a very eloquent trio on the physiology of blue curtains and bad characters—and swore eternal friendships over their muddy drinking water, and parted mutually comforted at each having found the only Socrates*

*of modern times in the other. To see people so perfectly
happy in this curious world is very interesting—I could
have blessed them from the bottom of my heart. . . .
[Mrs. Empson] said she had longed to see me to tell me
how happy she was. What joy there is on earth after
all, and I hope trouble never prevents anyone from
being glad in it, or makes them hang the world in
black because they have put on mourning.*[6]

Yet some of Flo's friends were in mourning. When
Clarkey lost a very dear friend, Flo tried to console her:

*All the world [is] putting on its shoes and stockings
every morning all the same, and the wandering earth
going its inexorable treadmill thro' these cold-hearted
stars in the Eternal Silence, as if nothing were the matter. . . . [But just as] Christ must go away before His
Spirit could come to His disciples, so I often fancy that
it is not till after the death of our friends that one can
have the most intimate union with their spirits.*[7]

Later Flo stressed the necessity of suffering:

*Oh, how I feel everything that you say, and that life
must seem to you now not worth the many tears. . . .
Indeed it seems to me as if a woman, suffer as she may,
never wishes it less. There are so many things, forgetful-
ness, thoughtlessness, which are more painful to her, that
she never asks herself whether this or that will bring
suffering or not. She would not avoid it if she could, and*

87

*like the penitent thief, who seems to have been the first
to understand that the Kingdom of Heaven was to be
entered upon through suffering, she seems to know intu-
itively that all her pleasure, affection, usefulness, sympathy, are to be had through suffering.*[8]

Flo became more and more introspective. She became
more disdainful of the frippery and finery of Mama's world.
Once, when she missed a ball, she thought how smashing
she would have been in her pink silk dress with the black lace
flounces. Then she caught herself. Such pride! Flo longed to
agree with 1 John: *For all that is in the world, the lust of the
flesh, and the lust of the eyes, and the pride of life, is not of the
Father, but is of the world.* "Pride of life" especially jolted her.
Pride. Pride. Pride. In her heart she knew she still indulged
"pride of life."

Flo adored John, the mystical disciple. She was herself
sensing more and more the unseen. After taking Communion
with a sick woman in the village, she later wrote:

*[I] suddenly felt that it was like the Upper Chamber
when the doors were shut, and He all at once stood in
the midst of them. He was the only reality there; she
herself and the others in the room were but ghosts who
put on form for a moment and would soon vanish into
invisibility.*[9]

But when the immediate sense of Christ's presence had
faded, Flo focused on the sick woman. This too was mystical. At that moment, Flo *knew* the woman was dying. She

was merely waiting to put on incorruption. Soon she would be a spirit.

God wants me, thought Flo, *to give her eyes, ears, and human reason to understand.*

And so she did.

She then wrote to Clarkey:

I think it is a mistake to say, as Carlyle does, that the end of life is to know ourselves and what we can do, because we may lose all interest in ourselves—so oftenest we wish to forget ourselves, but to know God and all His ways and all His intercourse with us, surely is the end of all our experience—and what really constitutes the "dark mystery" of life and its desolate emptiness is the veil which He has hung over His face. Oh the blessing of a pure heart, for it can only see God.[10]

To know God was all. Flo increasingly felt the presence of Christ. Yet, ironically, during this time she also saw more of Richard Monckton Milnes. She didn't attend his famous breakfast club, but Milnes came often to Embley Park, which Mama had relentlessly promoted into one of England's most sought-after invitations. All the other Nightingales were expected to recruit as well. Friends were expected to do likewise. Papa once wrote Clarkey to recruit the historian Leopold von Ranke, "Pray send him a sly line that he will find *notabilities* here."[11] Papa then listed Foreign Secretary Lord Palmerston, Speaker of the House Shaw Lefevre, and a number of other powerful guests, before adding with uncharacteristic haughtiness, "He should think well on this."[12]

At Embley Park, the "picked and chosen of society," as Mama immodestly phrased her guests, wandered sunny velvet-green grounds among laurels, rosebuds, and azaleas.[13] Obligated of course to entertain those guests was demure twenty-five-year-old Flo. Flo was not happy, nor was her confidante, Hilary, who had returned from Paris. Hilary was "at home" now and allowed only intermittent art lessons. The leisure of both young ladies was poisoned by knowing the true freedom Clarkey enjoyed. Flo's discontent worsened when Parthe, who enjoyed society immensely, began to needle her. She even chided Flo in letters to others, pointing out her gloominess and calling her "Foe."

Flo continued to daydream and feel guilty about it. Her spiritual quest had increased her sense of guilt in other ways too. "Wrongs" she had done others haunted her. She blamed her disagreeable relationship with Parthe on herself. New friendships tempted her into "crying on their shoulder." Or, worse yet, she was tempted to impress them with her "goodness." Her guilt and her temptations hung on her like chains. If only she could do something useful. But her constant yearning for good works became an object of guilt too. Was she motivated by a love of others or by a desire to escape a life that oppressed her? Yet she knew in her heart and mind that there was a world of sickness and poverty out there crying for help. But how would she—woman of privilege but also confinement—ever reach that pain? Her introspection and frustration were harder and harder to manage.

Even a letter to Hilary about a simple pleasure like her dog, Teazer, lapsed into morbid melancholy:

He came round the house and did not know me, but when I made the old sign he hesitated a moment and then came bounding up—with a welcome that gave me more pleasure than all the beauty [of the lovely grounds]. My dear Teazer, I love you better than all the nature in the world. How is it, my dear, that there is something so oppressive in inanimate and unconscious beauty that the only feeling there is sometimes, even when fully aware how glorious it is, is—let me be forgiven and let me die.[14]

Then Flo's despair really cried out in her letter:

I remember the voice which once said, "Be of good cheer, I have overcome the world," tho' to me it seemed only an echo for I have no courage for immortality; but it brings tears to my eyes when I remember how many have heard and felt that voice and. . .[bonded] themselves to their higher being.[15]

Other letters to Hilary were just as despondent:

I have walked up and down all these long summer evenings in the garden and could find no words but: My God, my God, why hast Thou forsaken me? How anyone can find ennui [boredom] in life I cannot think as it hurries along in what seems to me its wild, headlong course. . . . One feels as if one were carried by as if by a whirlwind and had no breath to connect anything, and could only just say: My days are now

past, my thoughts are broken off, and where is now my
hope?[16]

In another letter to Hilary, she expressed her guilt over
not answering God's call:

Oh, is our life here merely to deceive and be deceived? . . .
There are strange punishments here for those that have
made life consist of one idea and that one not God. . . .
I often feel how much truth there is in the old myths
of strange punishments and bewitchments. . .falling
on those who have defied the power of a God. . . . Oh,
dearest, pray for me—not for peace, for I have not suffi-
cient interest in myself to care about it; for what does it
signify? I can perform my duties as well at home with-
out it; indeed, I am more use to my father and mother
than I was five years ago—but for truth, truth, truth
and a manifestation of God.[17]

Meanwhile Mama fussed over her. "You know, my dear,
Lord Palmerston's daughter Fanny also was very restless.
He almost despaired. But she finally accepted reality and
stopped looking for the perfect man. Now as Lady Jocelyn,
she is so useful in society."

Flo knew perfectly well that Mama wanted her to
become Monckton Milnes's wife, a woman destined to be
Lady Houghton. Then at Lea Hurst that summer of 1845,
the Nightingales received word that Grandmama Shore was
gravely ill.

EIGHT

After the family visited Grandmama Shore at Tapton, Flo alone was allowed to stay on. Grandmama was partially paralyzed. Flo could do little that was therapeutic, but by now she knew very well how sick people appreciate the tiniest comforts. So she told her stories of the other grandchildren—Blanche, Shore, Bertha, and Beatrice. And, yes, even Parthe.

Grandmama bubbled with happiness. "Oh, my dear, when I think how many blessings I have, nothing can trouble me now!"[1]

Flo found peace of mind at Tapton. Caregiving was so satisfactory all the way around. Even problems seemed Godsent, if only she could be part of their solution, as caregiver or comforter. Grandmama Shore stabilized, much comforted by Flo. But suffering was everywhere for Flo, whether with Aunt Mai's depression over the lameness of one of her youngest daughters or with poor people in the village. Flo continued to visit the villages, often becoming intimately engrossed in their problems. One man she counseled had accidentally shot and killed his cousin. He was inconsolable. "How dreadful the afterlife of Cain must have been!" he would cry out suddenly.[2] Even the Nightingale household had its suffering. Their elderly family nursemaid became seriously ill at Lea Hurst. "Oh! I was so well, quite well till now. . . ," groaned the old servant.[3] But the elderly woman insisted on traveling south to Embley Park with the family. Once there, she lasted only two days. Had the trip killed her? Flo wrote to Hilary:

Our dear old friend had left us early that morning.
Her Father had sent for her so quietly that, though I
held her hand, I could not tell, except for the coldness,
the moment when her gallant spirit sped its way on its
noiseless journey. She suffered very much on Monday,
but on Tuesday it was all over before seven. Upright in
her chair she died. . .so short a time before her death her
voice was as strong as ever. . .now nothing in her room
to remind one of life excepting the tick of her watch,
and that stopped just before I came away. . . . [How
unpleasant] it is coming out of the room where there
is only her and God and me, to come back into the cold
and false life of prejudices and hypocrisy and conven-
tionalisms; by which I do not mean to find fault with
life but only with the use I make of it. It seems to me to
be all deceiving and vanitousness.[4]

There it was again: Flo's despair with the uselessness of her own life. God had called her nearly eight years before and still she did not know what to do nor how to do it! Clarkey had suggested writing novels as Jane Austen and other women had done. There was some freedom for women there. But Flo did not want to write plots of the mannered; after all, it was that polite society that smothered her. On the other hand, she certainly could not write steamy novels like George Sand, with whom she did not agree or approve. Oh Lord, what was she to do?

"Why do I not get another sign?"

After the death of her old nursemaid, Flo busied herself in the village of Wellow. Besides the usual deaths and births there was an unusual amount of sickness during the fall of 1845. Three times she was at deathbeds, almost an angelic presence awaiting the end. But one case made her realize that not every death was necessary.

Good heavens, her soul cried after one woman died, *they might as well have poured poison down her throat!*

Some of the poor people had notions about remedies that were not only false, but also deadly! In addition to that, all around her now she saw suffering that could be allevi-ated—perhaps even prevented—if only the caretakers knew what to do and how to do it. How outrageous it was to have to guess! Such treatment was irrational. Surely she was not the first to think of this paradox. Where could one get real medical training? She had taken many careful notes over the years about ailments and their remedies, but she was by no measure medically trained.

Then she recalled Dr. Fowler, a family friend. More than eighty years old, Dr. Fowler practiced medicine at the Salisbury Infirmary, a mere fifteen miles from Embley Park. The doctor would be a guest at Embley Park during the Christmas season. A plan began to grow in her mind. Why shouldn't she train at Salisbury under Dr. Fowler for several weeks? Then Flo could come back and give qualified care in the village. Not only could she serve, but she could teach oth-ers how to help. The more she thought about her idea, the more elaborate became her plan.

Someday, like Aunt Julia, she would be free of family. Then she would most assuredly take a small house in the village and start a Protestant "sisterhood" of caregivers—yes, like the one in Kaiserswerth that Christian Bunsen had talked about. Oh, if only she knew more about Kaiserswerth. If only she could start such an institution herself. What a boon for those who suffered! These thoughts were golden to her. All gloom evaporated. She felt heavenly. She could scarcely wait to broach the subject with Dr. Fowler at Christmastime.

"What an excellent thought," responded Dr. Fowler.

"But isn't that nursing?" screeched Mama as she overheard Flo's remarks to Dr. Fowler.

Flo remained calm. "Yes, in a sense. . ."

"Do you not know about nurses?" hissed Parthe. "They are all low and vulgar."

Parthe too? But Flo directed her calm toward Mama. "I'm sure the good doctor. . ."

But Mama was almost frantic. Flo had never seen her so irrational. "Nurses are common drunks," muttered Mama. "Do you wish to disgrace your family, Flo? How could you?"

Flo answered, "I've read Charles Dickens too, Mama. I know he paints a sordid picture of nurses. But I'm sure Dr. Fowler can assure you that caricature is poetic license."

Parthe snapped, "Don't you know most physicians are not gentlemen like Dr. Fowler? They will surely take advantage of you, Flo."

Dr. Fowler's mood had changed. "Perhaps it's best not to pursue this."

Dr. Fowler's wife echoed his advice. Flo had no ally now in her wonderful scheme. It was dead. She had avoided the use of the word "nurse"—but to no avail. After that defeat, Flo turned to theological treatises again for satisfaction. But the vehemence of Mama—and especially Parthe—ate at her. Why should their prejudices have to be hers? For that matter, why should their pleasures have to be hers? She did not begrudge them their pleasures. Papa, too, disappointed her. Would he never stand up to Mama? Or did he agree with Mama that Flo's pursuit—her grand dream of fulfillment—was degrading?

"I must go into London," announced Papa after New Year's Day of 1846. "Parliament is going to debate the Corn Laws. Keeping a tariff on imported grain seems especially cruel now that the Irish and some of our own English are suffering from the potato blight."

Flo had to wonder whether Papa was merely escaping the strife at Embley Park. He was less and less connected to the family. Mama ran everything now. And Parthe was her shadow. After Papa went into London to stay with Aunt Jane, Flo was at Mama's beck and call—and Parthe's. It was certainly no consolation to Flo that Hilary, also at Aunt Jane's, wrote how much she enjoyed dining with Thomas Macauley and in general being immersed in all the politics and literature of London. Hilary also noted that Flo's father complained of England's unfulfilled young ladies. They did not know what to do with themselves, he said.

"But now I do know!" muttered Flo as she read the letter. "And why don't you do something about it, Papa? If our Savior walked the earth now and I went to Him, would He send me back to this life I am leading? No. He would say to me, 'Do this work for Me!'"

Flo agonized more and more over her dilemma. God had called her. And she did nothing, although now she was more sure of what she should do. Oh, she knew what Mama and Parthe were saying: "Why does she think she is so special?

Her desires are no more than vanity and selfishness." Perhaps Papa felt the same way. It all appeared so hopeless. It was during this time that Flo found another trusted confidante in Selina Bracebridge of Coventry.

By letter of introduction, the Bracebridges had sent the Howes to Embley Park. Flo's pet name for Selina became "Sig," shortened from *sigma,* the Greek letter for S. Sig was a close friend of Clarkey's too, so it was little wonder that Sig understood completely what Flo was suffering. But could Sig help her? Flo soon realized that Selina Bracebridge was the strongest willed of all her confidantes. She offered not just sympathy but strategies. And she was sly enough to stay on the good side of Mama and Parthe—yet be in complete sympathy with Flo. But as yet Sig could not see a way out for Flo either.

In June, when Flo returned for the summer stay in Lea Hurst, she noted wearily in her journal:

Arrived here tonight. Everything the same. . .yet how much one has thought and suffered since one was last here. All my plans have been wrecked and my hopes destroyed, and yet without any visible, any material change. . . . Our movements are so regular that our year is more marked even than other people's, and often the year returns without having had any visible fruit of all its tribulation but experience. . .and the experience how sad. However, I must not belie St. Paul, who, I believe, saves his truth by saying that it is the experience of patience which worketh hope.[5]

Yes, hope was one of the three great Christian virtues. She must never give up hope, or faith, or love. So she buoyed herself in hope, writing, "The longer I live, the more I feel as if all my being was gradually drawing to one point."[6] Yet she fluctuated back and forth between that hope and despair. To Hilary, she wrote:

My life is so full of anxieties, of eager fears about these things which are inextricable, things about which I really don't know which I wish, that I kneel down when the sun rises in the morning, & only say, Behold the handmaiden of the Lord, give me this day any work, no not my work, but Thine to do. I ask no other blessing.[7]

How tedious the whole process was, how melancholy, perhaps even self-pitying. *Lord, free me from this,* she prayed. She read the Bible and Homer. She had little use for novels at this time of her life, often setting aside her reading and thinking of angels. Wouldn't one come with a message for her? She meditated more and more. Lying in bed in an upper-floor bedroom at Lea Hurst one night, she gazed at a flickering candle. The candle was like human reason, she thought. Its glare prevented her from seeing the moonlit landscape outside her window. That invisible landscape was the spiritual world—yes, the real world.

She made July 7 her self-examination day. This self-appraisal was profoundly depressing. She realized how much the family consumed her. Much, if not all, of her activity was trivial. She had resumed her Greek lessons to please Papa.

She also rode with him in the hills to give him companionship. Each day she had to read her friends' letters aloud to Mama. Mama also had her reading novels aloud for her. Flo always had to be ready to amuse poor, sensitive Parthe. Lately, Flo had been reading a novel aloud to her too. And each day Flo wrote letters to her friends, often lamenting her own woes. She regretted her complaining. It was vanity.

"Oh, what a worm I am," Flo admitted to herself bitterly.

But then there was the nearby village of Holloway. In its gabled, gray-stone cottages hugging the hill slopes, her heart filled once again with purpose. For a while she felt as if she only existed to relieve the suffering of those poor unfortunates. On July 16, she wrote in her journal:

I can do without marriage. . .or any of the things that people sigh after. My imagination is so filled with the misery of the world, that the only thing worth trouble seems to me to be helping or sympathizing there—the only thing where labor brings any return. When I am driving about a town, all the faces I see seem to me either anxious or depressed or diseased, and my soul flings itself forth to meet them, to "pledge them in the cup of grief." My mind is absorbed with the idea of the sufferings of man, it besets me behind and before. A very one-sided view, but I can hardly see anything else, and all the poets sing of the glories of this world seems to me untrue. All the people I see are eaten up with care or poverty or disease. When I go into a cottage, I long to stop there all day, to wash the children,

relieve the mother, stay by the sick one. And behold
there are a hundred other families unhappy within
half a mile.[8]

Yes! This was her calling—caring for the suffering. She knew that now. At long last, she was certain! Two days later, she wrote in her journal:

It satisfies my soul, it supplies every want of my heart
and soul and mind. It heals all my disease. It redeems
my life from destruction. . . . I want nothing else, my
heart is filled. I am at home. I want no other heaven.
I can desire no further benefits, as long as Evil has its
reign in the world.[9]

Unfortunately for Flo, the Nightingales were soon heading south again. It tore at Flo's heart to leave her "patients" in Holloway. Two boys dying of consumption she knew she would never see again. "Goodbye, poor people, for ten months. Goodbye," she wrote wistfully in her journal.[10] Back at Embley Park, as a part of her voracious reading, Flo studied reports on prison reform. She approved some kind of rehabilitation. She had seen the squalor and hopelessness that the poor had to fight. Of course her own great privilege—which she did nothing to merit—made her feel even worse. By now she knew her father's annual income was not much less than Queen Victoria's!

She had another jolt. None other than Richard Monckton Milnes had introduced a bill in Parliament to establish juvenile reformatories, so that the youths would not be thrown in with grizzled criminals. Milnes had surprised everyone by getting elected to Parliament. And he had not settled into being "clubby" about it. He had traveled to Ireland to see the consequences of the potato famine. He was an activist. He also came to Embley Park with ever greater frequency.

"My mother is dying in Brighton," Milnes told Flo, "and no one comforts me more than you."

Milnes had grown in Flo's eyes. His attention now thrilled her. Could she satisfy her restlessness with such an active man? Or would she become like Mama, merely the chief instigator of all his social activity? And what of her "call"? Wasn't it clear now that she was destined to do something in the medical realm? If only she could be Milnes's closest friend and confidante—but not his wife. But such cerebral relationships between men and women were almost impossible in England.

Meanwhile her relationship with Sig grew. Of Mrs. Bracebridge, Flo wrote in her journal:

I wonder whether she knows what a difference she has made in my life. The very fact of there being one person by whom one's thoughts are not pronounced fit only for a dream not worth disputing, who does not look upon one as a fanciful spoilt child who ought to take life as it is and enjoy it—that mere fact changes the whole aspect of things to one. Since one has found that there is one person who does not think that Society ought to make one happy, I have never had that sinking of spirits at the thought of the three winter months of

perpetual row. . . . But in general I do think that we
ought to seek sympathy for what we do, not for what
we suffer; except in cases of overwhelming agony,
when our Saviour himself needed an angel from
heaven.[11]

Nevertheless, Sig did ask Flo whether she could not find happiness in marriage as she herself had. Flo told her bluntly she believed God "has as clearly marked out some to be single women as he has others to be wives, and has organized them accordingly for their vocation." The truth was that, at twenty-six, Flo had almost resolved not to marry. But sometimes she was overwhelmed by guilt. Was she just putting on a show of purity and good intentions? In her journal, she wrote:

Lord sanctify to me Sig's friendship—let it not mislead
me to represent before her, but let me think more of her
approbation as it will be when she knows me spirit to
spirit than as it is while she only knows me face to face.
And if I have any other dangerous friendship, which
leads me to vanity, do Thou, Lord, purify it and defend
me.—Oh, God, no more love. No more marriage,
O God.[12]

Flo steeled herself. She had heard a thousand com-ments—all derogatory—about how Fanny, Lord Palmerston's very difficult daughter, had resisted marriage. So Flo had no illusions about being admired for her desire to be different. But the truth was that now she felt far more guilt about the neglect shown by the upper class to the poor and the sick. *I am like the poor now*, she thought. *We expect little from life, much from God.* Oh, how the poor trusted Flo. "I can tell you everything the same as if you were my mother," said one poor woman.[13] What a magnificent responsibility for Flo. Why, it was a thousand times more important than her social obligations to the upper class. And to think that in her own house she was treated like a confused child!

Her thoughts became angrier:

> *This house is the embodiment to me of the drainage of the poor to fill the rich, who, upon the plea of a better bonnet and a better dinner, blurt out "truths" to the poor and expect them to be grateful (without knowing their manners, hardly even their language, certainly not their feelings). . . . I loathe that house.*[14]

Surely these fiery thoughts come from God, she thought. He was sending this heat to Flo until she did His will. On the other hand, if they were not from God, they would die out. But they strengthened. On December 31, 1846, she wrote:

> *It has often been said: How extraordinary that Jesus Christ should have arisen among the working class! But how much, much more extraordinary if He were to arise among our class. Nay, almost beyond a miracle for Him ever to come to see us. We have no time! . . . We're too busy—we have no time for that (prayer). . .which our Saviour found so necessary that He sat up whole*

nights for it, having so much to do in the day.[15]

During the daytime, Flo toiled in the muddy lanes of Wellow more and more. Long before dawn, she awoke to study reports. Evenings were almost a dead loss, because she had to sit in the drawing room—young lady-in-waiting—until ten o'clock. She salvaged some of the evenings by retreating into her dreams, not so fuzzy now that Christian Bunsen had sent her a detailed report of the Kaiserswerth Institute. This report confirmed exactly what Flo wished to do in England. Young Protestant maidens served the Lord by nursing and teaching the poor. And after many years, the Kaiserswerth Institute had even been recognized by the Prussian government.

Then a remarkable thought jolted Flo. Why found her own institute in England? Why could she not join the Kaiserswerth Institute? But oh how Mama—and her shadow Parthe—would fight her. Defiantly she wrote in her journal:

> *Resignation. . . I never understood that word. It does not occur once in the Bible. . . . Our Saviour never resigned Himself. And in all the great sufferings which I have seen, I have never felt inclined to say, "Resign yourself," but [to] Overcome.*[16]

Meanwhile, her men friends were changing England. Lord Ashley's Ten-Hours Bill finally was passed into law in May 1847. The future Lord Shaftsbury, Lord Ashley, had fought for many years to protect women and children.

Meanwhile, the thrust and parry of "why doesn't Flo marry?" never stopped. Richard Monckton Milnes was more persistent than ever. Then Flo was shocked to learn that Clarkey had married the brilliant Egyptologist Julius Mohl, a German but longtime resident of Paris. Flo had met Julius and knew he was just right for Clarkey. At the age of fifty or so, Clarkey had married. Was it then not still possible for Flo? Should she reward Monckton Milnes for his patient courtship? She searched her heart.

"When I imagine myself as his wife, I am overwhelmed with unhappiness," Flo confided in Sig.

Then at long last, Sig justified Flo's great faith in her.

NINE

Sig hit upon a wonderful scheme to get Flo away from her social bondage—for a while. When the Bracebridges decided to go to Rome for the winter, they invited Flo to go with them. Winter was the time of the most intense stress between Flo and her family. Flo thanked God for Sig's social skills, because Mama and Papa had complete faith in her too. They agreed without hesitation. Not even Parthe was upset. In fact, she busied herself dictating just what wardrobe Flo would take and just exactly which people Flo must call on once there.

"Rome will rest her mind," Parthe condescendingly confided to her friends, implying that Flo was a very troubled person indeed.

Flo and the Bracebridges arrived in Rome the evening of November 9, 1847. They stayed near the Piazza del Popolo. The next day, long before dawn, Flo awakened, exulting in the thought of seeing St. Peter's Cathedral. Finally, she could not wait for the Bracebridges to arise. She walked furiously along the streets, looking neither left nor right. As she entered St. Peter's Square, framed by its stunning colonnades, the sun was just touching the cathedral. At the entrance, she gathered herself, breath, and mind. As she wrote her family later:

No event in my life, except my death, can ever be greater
than the first entrance into St. Peter's. . . . I could not
have gone there for the first time except alone; no, not in

*the company of St. Peter himself. . . . There was hardly
a creature there but I. There I knelt down. . .it was
the effect of the presence of God. . . . The side chapels
are like small churches in themselves. . . . The Pieta (by
Michelangelo) was within a yard of the place I expected
to find it.[1]*

When Flo left the cathedral, she was struck by how
bitterly cold the air was. She had felt nothing on her way
there. For several weeks after that day, Flo was a relentless
sightseer. She followed an itinerary Papa had designed for
her, ticking off each sight after she visited it. She was happier than she had thought she would ever be again. Always
she was drawn back to St. Peter's and the Vatican. One day,
in the Vatican's Sistine Chapel, she saw Michelangelo's
supreme masterpiece, his depiction of the Old Testament
on the enormous ceiling. It had been done in fresco, the
most challenging form of art in that it was painted on fresh
plaster each day. Revision was virtually impossible. Only
the greatest master could attempt such a thing. To Flo, it
was the zenith of human art. She wrote:

*Think of a day alone in the Sistine Chapel with Sig—
quite alone. . .without visitors—looking up into that
heaven of angels and prophets. . .we began to praise
God. Oh my dear, for words to describe those figures—
but there are none, except the words of the men
themselves with the prophecies—there they are, each
breathing the very spirit they had breathed in life and
handed down to us. . . . I did not think I was looking*

*at pictures, but looking into Heaven itself. . .and the
blackening of the colors were the dimness of my own
earthly vision. . . . There are few moments which we
shall carry with us through the gate of Death. . .but
this I am sure will be one of mine. . . . [The figures] are
almost too wonderful for mortal eyes.*[2]

Flo was enraptured with Isaiah, whose writings she
regarded more highly than Shakespeare's. For Flo, Isaiah
was the forerunner of Christ. And she was absolutely certain that Michelangelo had captured the true Isaiah. Yet she
did not enjoy seeing Michelangelo's *Last Judgment* on the
wall behind the altar. She had even hoped the failing afternoon light in the chapel would prevent her seeing the Lord
separating the "sheep" from the "goats." But no. Flo could
see it all too clearly. This fresco had been just as demanding, with just as dazzling results. But it was depressing, even
frightening to Flo. Michelangelo had wanted it so. In the
fresco, even St. Peter has fear in his eyes. Eternal damnation
awaits some! Flo did not want to believe this.

She and Sig had been in the Sistine Chapel nearly all day.
She was glad when they left. Away from the chapel, Flo let
the great ceiling dominate her thoughts. Eternal damnation
she suppressed.

Rome was truly a delight. She even enjoyed socializing again. One of the first couples Flo met in Rome was
the immensely wealthy Herberts of Wilton, only twenty
miles from Embley Park. Flo should not have liked Sidney
Herbert much, for after all, he was a Tory and very High
Church, leaning toward the Catholic traditions. However,

she found him not only gracious but sincere in his intentions to do good. He wielded power in the government too, as Peel's secretary of war. His wife, Elizabeth, was just as open and friendly. Flo wrote home, praising Sidney Herbert as "so little like a man of the world," and Elizabeth, "the sunshine of Italy."[3]

Flo welcomed 1848, luxuriating in the grandeur of Rome. But her enjoyment began to wear on her even there. Could she ignore Roman urchins, begging everywhere on the streets, all desperately poor? Why could she not help some of them as she helped children at Wellow and Holloway? It was not long before she had virtually assumed responsibility for a little girl named Felicetta Sensi. Attempting to arrange the education of this child caused Flo to be summoned by Mother Santa Colomba at the Convent of the Trinita dei Monti.

"The Mother is going to tell me to leave Felicetta alone," worried Flo.

But no. The Mother could not have been kinder. Flo was summoned because the convent ran an orphan school. They would take the child in, but they requested 180 scudi for five years. As wealthy as William Nightingale was, Flo had little money for her own use. Where could she get such a sum? Mulling it over, she decided the money would come out of her clothing allowance. So Flo signed a contract, assuring the child an education. But she avoided talking about her act of charity. That would have made it appear she did it only to make herself look noble.

The incident had another result. Mother Santa Colomba recognized Flo's ravenous spiritual hunger. She encouraged her to participate in the convent. Flo tried it, studying the rule of their Order of the Sacred Heart and trying to understand how these women dealt with the trials of life. Mother Santa Colomba, in bad health and often in pain, insisted this affliction was sent to her by God. She accepted it, just as St. Paul had finally accepted the "thorn in his side," with joy. She would die laughing, she told Flo. The only thing—"*unicamente!*"—was to do the will of God. And for her that was to educate the orphans of Rome.

"But how am I to know what His will is for me?" blurted Flo.

"Pray. Ask God, 'Am I to do Your will in a religious order or in the world? If in the world, married or single?'" Then the nun added, "God generally answers."

Flo admired her candor. Mother Santa Colomba had not guaranteed an answer. Ever methodical, Flo recorded everything she saw and heard at the convent, including how the children were educated. The latter information she might use at Wellow. The atmosphere of this orphan school was unlike the clamor and harshness of English schools. The nuns created an atmosphere of calm. The children came in defiant and unruly. Soon they were almost angelic!

"Teachers must be lighthearted," insisted Mother Santa Colomba, "to create an atmosphere of loving kindness."

Flo was shocked to see the little "angels" contradict their teachers. Even the teaching sisters contradicted Mother Santa Colomba. Yet freedom made love blossom everywhere. Flo's idea of oppressive dogma in the Catholic world had been wrong. The children said only short prayers.

"Say less and understand more," explained Mother Santa Colomba.[4]

Flo, too, was encouraged to criticize. She had been swallowing all her criticism but now spoke out in front of the entire community. The sisters indulged in too many vocal prayers, she said. The sisters accepted her criticism, although one said Flo was a donkey in her spiritual development. Flo rejoiced in the blunt comment! Flo loved the nuns' character, their joyous way of service. Increasingly she compared Mother Santa Colomba to her friend Sig. The two represented the very best women produced by the Protestant and Catholic faiths. They both thought only of pleasing others, never themselves. She revered them both.

But Flo confided to Mother Santa Colomba, "I feel like such a failure."

Mother Santa Colomba told her she must accept failure. God knew she had failed. She must be as joyous in failure as she was in success. It all came from God. Being anxious or miserable pleased no one. Should Flo expect more "success" than the Lord? He was thwarted by everyone in His earthly mission. Even His own apostles understood little of who He was before the Resurrection. And finally, the nun told Flo she had prayed about her many times. She was sure that God was not calling her to become Catholic. But Flo must turn her whole heart to God so that she would be ready to do His will. The nun was certain that Flo was called to do something very special! Then Flo received an exceptional gift from Mother Santa Colomba. She was allowed to make a retreat at the convent. After the retreat, she recorded her final conversation with the nun:

> *Mother SC: Did not God speak to you during this retreat? Did He not ask you anything?*
>
> *Flo: He asked me to surrender my will.*
>
> *Mother SC: And to whom?*
>
> *Flo: To all that is upon the earth.*
>
> *Mother SC: He calls you to a very high degree of perfection. Take care. If you resist, you will be very guilty.*[5]

Vowing to crush her self-will so that she could do only the will of God, Flo said goodbye to her friends in the convent. The Bracebridges and Flo left Rome at the beginning of April. What had affected her more? God revealed through Michelangelo? Or God revealed through a pious nun? Why weigh the difference? Rome had been wonderful. Italy itself was still parceled out and fighting for liberty and unity, but Flo had never been less interested. Still, by habit she called herself a friend of united Italy, and united Germany, or any people united for liberty.

This idealism upset Parthe. "Foreigners are scarcely likely to know what to do with freedom anyway," she sniffed.

Parthe was certainly not alone in her sentiment. She shared the consensus of the "picked and chosen" who strolled the rose-bordered garden paths of Embley Park. "Such arrogance," fumed Flo. Soon she was arguing with Mama, sparring with Parthe. It angered her that Papa, who agreed with her, made himself scarce. Then Flo realized she had resumed all her old angers. Enduring Parthe—and Mama too—had seemed so simple in the convent. Now at Embley

Park, crushing her self-will appeared impossible. How could she do that around people who bullied her? Wouldn't that just mean she would never be able to do the will of God? Oh, how she longed for the peace of the convent and the comfort of like minds.

At least she was allowed to work in the school at Wellow—even instituting some things she had learned at the orphan school in Rome. But so too did she endure her monotonous evenings in the drawing room at Embley Park, as well as Mama's never-ending social whirl. How unreal their life at Embley Park was.

In an English country place, everything that is painful is so carefully removed out of sight, behind those fine trees to a village three miles off, and all the intercourse with your fellow creatures is that between the landlord and his tenant, the dependent and the dependee, the untruest possible.[6]

In spite of her feelings of futility, she renewed her confidences with Aunt Julia, Aunt Mai, and Hilary. She cultivated her newer friendships: Sig, of course, but also Elizabeth Herbert. Mrs. Herbert, besides being a new mother, was founding a convalescent home at Charmouth. So she was doing what she could within the confines of marriage. The Herberts were Tories, so Flo began to suspect perhaps there was not that much difference in the political parties after all. Queen Victoria had recently come to the same conclusion. Before her marriage to Prince Albert, the tiny, hot-tempered queen had been staunchly Whig. Now it appeared she was leaning toward the Tories. Were Flo and dreamy-eyed Papa being fools to think the political parties were different? Were both parties merely representing the well-to-do, with only the smallest shades of difference?

"Am I going to spend the rest of my life becoming more and more disillusioned?" she commented wearily.

Then Flo learned that Clarkey and her husband, Julius Mohl, had gone to Frankfurt, Germany, to escape political turmoil in Paris. God would not turn France upside down to please Flo, but it was fortuitous. Frankfurt was very near Kaiserswerth! Flo could visit the Mohls in order to visit the Protestant deaconesses at the Kaiserswerth Institute. But Frankfurt itself was soon in turmoil. So that plan—and any vain notion about God's arranging it for her—evaporated.

When the social cycle took her again to London, Flo found good works there to escape to during the day. The reformer Lord Ashley had been promoting for six years what were called "ragged schools" for poor children. By 1849, ragged schools numbered eighty-eight. Of the almost one thousand volunteer teachers, one was Flo. Some of these teachers had the same joy of the teaching she saw at the orphan school in Rome. Of one she wrote:

He has the whole hundred little thieves like one soul moved by his breath. I never spent so delightful an hour in my life. . . . There are Michelangelos of different kinds in God's creation and this man was rearing as harmonious and perfect an invisible dome toward heaven out of the stones and lifeless hearts around him as the great architect himself in the greatest wonder of

Christian architecture. God be praised that these mar-
vels do not cease.[7]

Life was raw in London. One could see people dying on the streets. Now there was a monstrous problem crying out for her help. It pleased her to educate, she finally admitted to herself, but it did not bring joy. No, teaching was not her calling. And her daydreams had returned. All would admire her, she fancied in her dreams. She still had visions of personal success! How she loathed her own ambition, her restlessness, just as others did.

"It's all so tiresome," she admitted.

During the summer of 1849, the Bracebridges introduced Flo to a young woman her same age named Elizabeth Blackwell. Elizabeth had the same fire in her that Flo had. A woman could not attend medical school in England, so Elizabeth had gone to medical school in America! Now she was a certified physician but still unable to practice in England. She only visited England before going to Paris for more training. Eventually she would return to America to practice medicine. Every step of the way, she had been supported by her father in Bristol. Flo had nothing but admiration for Elizabeth Blackwell's determination, but the more she thought about her own family's lack of support—especially now Papa's—the more depressed she became!

Once again, the Bracebridges sought to remove her from her unhappiness. This winter they were going to Egypt. Would Flo come?

But before she could do anything else, she had to face another quandary. Richard Monckton Milnes pursued her everywhere now: Embley Park, London, Lea Hurst. He wanted an answer. Would she marry him or not? This time, he said it with finality. As much as he wanted her, he could wait no longer. He was nearly forty, Flo nearly thirty. She had to admit his stature grew in her eyes every day. He was now established as a liberal Whig, espousing the very ideals Flo loved. He worked on a biography of the poet John Keats. Why could she not love this gifted Monckton Milnes? She couldn't bear the thought of his one day giving up on her. Was she going to force him to give up on her so that she could preserve her ambition—an ambition that had so little chance of ever happening?

She told him, "I cannot marry you." Her heart remained closed to him.

With that rejection, Mama was furious. She didn't care whether Flo left the country or not. In November 1849, Flo arrived with the Bracebridges at Alexandria, Egypt. She had prepared herself well. She knew some very distinguished Egyptologists in Christian Bunsen and Julius Mohl. She took a small library with her about Egypt. She was determined to take Egypt—called in some circles the "East"—and its ancient mysteries by storm. And with good cheer too. In Alexandria, she fired a lively letter off to Embley Park:

> *Yes, my dear people, I have set my first footfall in the East and oh! that I could tell you the new world of old poetry, of Bible images of light, and life, and beauty which that word opens. My first day in the East, and it has been one of the most striking, I am sure—one can never forget through Eternity.*[8]

In Alexandria, Flo was taken inside a mosque—such a terrible affront to Muslims that she had to be heavily disguised. If they had known the masked intruder was a woman, they might have killed her. In another letter home, she would write that the perilous visit to the mosque revealed "what it is to be a woman in these countries, where Christ has not been to raise us. God save them, for it is a hopeless life."[9] Although Cairo stunned her with its alien beauty, the human misery she saw was so appalling she had to turn away and thank God she did not have to stay.

But the worst scene was the surrounding desert. She wrote, "One goes riding out, and one really feels inclined to believe this is the kingdom of the devil."[10]

Up the Nile she toured by ship. As much as she was supposed to admire the pyramids—which they saw from a distance but had not yet visited—she loathed them. She could imagine nothing more vulgar, having nothing to commend them but size and resistance to time. But Egypt was choked with other relics that had also resisted time. So what did the pyramids represent? To Flo they represented tyranny—vain objects built by breaking the backs of slaves!

Frequently they docked and the passengers went ashore to explore. Flo and the Bracebridges had their own escort, Paolo, a very experienced guide of about fifty. To Flo, the desert continued to be diabolical, the killer of life. Ruins were everywhere. "One almost fancies one hears the devil laughing," she wrote.[11] Was it any wonder Christ encountered the devil in the desert? The desert constantly reminded her of the struggle between God and Satan. Egypt was fast becoming a potent experience for her, a religious experience.

One day aboard ship, they were struck by a sandstorm so violent that dunes of sand ran across the surface of the Nile. What a sight! Once, in a storm, a boat went careening helplessly past their ship. The wind never let up in its fury until the next morning. Then the entire day they were drenched with rain. When the storm passed, they learned four boats had gone down, every passenger lost. Who could doubt anything in Genesis and Exodus after these violent episodes?

Her letters were no longer perky:

Everything in Egypt is so inexpressibly solemn; nothing ever laughs or plays here. . . . Everything is grown up and grown old. One never sees creatures at play here as in other countries. . . . I have seen nothing pretty since we left Cairo. . .[the Arab crew] are despairing, indifferent, that is all. If Paolo says, "How far is it to Girgeh?" "God knows." "But how soon shall we get there?" "When God pleases." "But I ask how many hours it is, because the master wants to put it down in his journal?" "God knows."[12]

The mud huts of the Arabs appalled her:

To see human beings choosing darkness rather than light, building their doorways four feet high or less, choosing to crawl upon the ground like reptiles, to live in a place where they could not stand upright. . . . In a cold climate, one could have understood it; but here it seemed as if they did it on purpose to be as like beasts as they could. . . . If they had been deserted, you would have thought it was the dwelling-place of some wild animal. I never before saw any of my fellow creatures [so] degraded.[13]

Finally their ship arrived at Thebes, where they could go ashore to explore the grand ruins of Karnak, of Luxor, and of the Valley of Kings. Flo focused her reason and all her preparation for Egypt on this exploration and subsequent long, erudite letters. But in her heart and soul, Flo was profoundly disturbed by Egypt and its satanic desert.

TEN

Flo wrote of the desert "being perpetually restless, of Milton's Satan, turning ceaselessly from side to side in his lake of fire."[1] Another time she described the desert as "a great dragon, putting out his fiery tongue and licking up the green, fertile plain, biting into it."[2] She was frank in her letters, but not as frank as she was in a tiny diary she started on New Year's Day of 1850. Entries in her diary revealed the true depth of her turmoil, "day-dreaming" in her mind being a killer of action:

> *1 Jan—*
> *(at Luxor) Dreaming...*
>   *17 Jan—*
> *(at Abu Simbel) Dreamed in the very face of God.*
>   *20 Jan—*
> *(in temple cave) Oh heavenly fire, purify me—free me from this slavery.*
>   *22 Jan—*
> *By the temple of Isis with the roar of the Cataract, I thought I should see Him. His shadow in the moon-light...*
>   *26 Jan—*
> *(at Janeb) I spoiled it all with dreaming. Disappointed with myself & the Effect of Egypt on me. Rome was better.*
>   *27 Jan—*
> *(on Sunday) Took my crucifix up before breakfast to lay*

it in the sacred dust of the Chamber of Osiris. Prayers. . .

   11 Feb—

Did not go out—but the demon of dreaming had possession of my weakened head. . .

   16 Feb—

Karnak—& where was I? All the while. . .dreaming. . .[3]

In late February, the life of her soul became truly mystical. God began speaking through the words of Mother Santa Colomba:

   22 Feb—

Long morning by myself. . .on the steps of Portico. . . God spoke to me once again. . .

   28 Feb—

(Tombs of the Kings) God called me with. . .[Mother Santa Colomba's] words.

   3 Mar—

Did not get up in the morning, but God gave me the time. . .to "meditate" on. . .[Mother Santa Colomba's] words.

   7 Mar—

God called me in the morning and asked me would I do good for Him, for Him alone without the reputation.

   8 Mar—

Thought much upon. . .[Mother Santa Colomba's] words], "Can you hesitate between the God of the whole Earth & your little reputation?"[4]

10 Mar—

Every day, during the quarter of an hour I had by myself, after dinner & after breakfast, in my own cabin, read. . .[Mother Santa Colomba's] words—Can you give up the reputation of suffering much & saying little? they cried to me.

15 Mar—

God has delivered me from the great offence—& the constant murderer of my thoughts.

16–17 Mar—

(in Cairo) God told me what a privilege He had reserved for me. . .Kaiserswerth. . . . If I were never thinking of the reputation, how I should be better able to see what God intends for me.

What a spiritual experience! After Egypt and its terrible desert tormented her mind, God had talked to her! God had raised the promise of Kaiserswerth. The process really defied human understanding. But she was more sure than ever that Kaiserswerth held the answer for her. As if to confirm it, just before she left Egypt she visited a dispensary in Alexandria run by Christian sisters who took no vows. As the sisters tended hundreds of poor Arabs, their joy radiated from them.

Yet after leaving Egypt to visit Greece, Flo's spirits sank again. Surely Kaiserswerth was just a dream itself. Hadn't it been eight years since Christian Bunsen had first suggested it? Why did she think Kaiserswerth would materialize now? But in Greece she had a significant event. Would it be pivotal for her?

> *12 May—*
> *Today I am thirty—the age Christ began His mission.*
> *Now no more childish things, no more vain things, no*
> *more love, no more marriage. Now, Lord, let me think*
> *only of Thy Will, what Thou willest me to do—Oh*
> *Lord Thy Will, Thy Will.*[5]

She tried desperately to crush her own ambition:

> *18 May—*
> *My history. . .[is] a history of miserable woe, mistake,*
> *and blinding vanity, of seeking great things for myself.*
> *19 May—*
> *God, I place myself in Thy Hands. . . . If it be Thy Will*
> *that I should go on suffering, let it be so. . . .*
> *21 May—*
> *Let me only accomplish the Will of God. Let me not*
> *desire great things for myself. . . .*
> *10 June—*
> *The Lord spoke to me: He said, "Give five minutes*
> *every hour to the thought of Me. . . ."*[6]

Still, Flo sank deeper into depression. By the end of June, she could scarcely believe her eyes. The handwriting in her diary was that of an old lady. Was she so heartsick she was dying? *Oh, please save me, God,* she prayed.

Suddenly she was apprised of Sig's brilliant strategy. On the overland route back to England, they would detour in Germany—where at last Flo would visit Kaiserswerth! And yet, Flo felt no joy at all. In fact, she was so apprehensive that this last hope would disappoint her, she was almost paralyzed. Feebly she wrote:

> 9 July—
> *I did not think it worthwhile to get up in the morning. What could I do but offend God?. . .on the brink of accomplishing my greatest wish. . . . I seemed to be unfit, unmanned for it—it seemed not to be the calling for me [after all]. . . . I did not feel the spirit, the energy for doing anything at Kaiserswerth. . . .*[7]

Suppose she indeed discovered Kaiserswerth was not her calling? Could she handle a disappointment as enormous as that? Was there any hope beyond Kaiserswerth? In despair, she wrote that she was "lost and past redemption, a slave that could not be set free."[8] With her traveled a small menagerie she had collected in her calmer moments in Greece: a pair of tortoises named Mr. and Mrs. Hill, a cicada dubbed Plato, and a baby owl she called Athena. In Czechoslovakia, Athena ate Plato. This tiny tragedy foreshadowed another period of intense despair that hit Flo as she neared Kaiserswerth.

"However, I have no choice but to visit," she said despondently.

In such a state of mind, she arrived at Kaiserswerth on July 31. Pastor Fliedner and his wife ignored her funk. Energetic and cheerful, the Fliedners appeared overjoyed to show her their institute. Flo was mildly pleased when they insisted she stay in the quarters with the Protestant deaconesses. She had seen nothing yet and felt strange confined in a tiny room that first night. Then Flo was amazed to feel her heart soar again. Surely this was what God intended! The next morning, she was actually helping Sister Katerina bathe a group of boisterous children in the orphanage. Later she observed the sister as she taught the children in the school. Then Flo stayed until long after midnight with a deaconess who nursed in the hospital. Every hour they patrolled the wards together. The wards were squeaky clean, with none of the foul smells usually endured in hospitals. And everything was completely proper. The deaconesses nursed only female patients. Males attended male patients.

All patients received spiritual help as well as medical care. Every facet of the Fliedner institution was carried out in this spirit. The children in the orphanage and the infant school were subjected to both academic and biblical learning. One day, Flo was fortunate to see how a new orphan was welcomed. The welcome was like a joyous birthday party. Pastor Fliedner presided, encouraging the new child to choose the songs to be sung. The child even received a modest gift. The welcome ended with all the children joining in to pray for the latest foundling.

"The love in this place is overwhelming," sighed Flo.

Wayward young women were also housed at Kaiserswerth. They too were treated with kindness. Unlike other institutions of the day, Kaiserswerth did not give them tedious sewing to occupy endless hours. The young women gardened and did various farm chores. Flo was thrilled to see how the women responded to farm animals. One very bitter looking newcomer melted when she was allowed to milk the cows. She actually danced for joy.

Flo carefully noted the way the Fliedners managed the institute. She could find no fault, other than suspecting that their medical practices were not up-to-date. But that was due to a lack of doctors. Everything else was perfect. Piety. Cleanliness. Love. Discipline. Work. Trust. She could not have been more at peace. Her joy was unbounded. The only comparison she could think of was John Bunyan's "House Beautiful" in *The Pilgrim's Progress*.

"Come in, thou blessed of the Lord, this house was built by the Lord of the Hill. . . ," remembered Flo of the welcome to travelers in Bunyan's classic allegory.

For two weeks she had been allowed to observe. When she left for England, she was ebullient, "feeling so brave as if nothing could ever vex me again."[9] Pastor Fliedner had asked Flo to write a report on his institute so the English people would know of their work. She was so focused that she wrote a thirty-two-page tract—specifically for other English women like herself—that described the "Institution of Kaiserswerth on the Rhine for the Practical Training of Deaconesses, under the direction of the Reverend Pastor Fliedner." Here was an opportunity for all in England like herself to escape the busy idleness in which they were confined at home.

"Oh, England's miserable underused women," she lamented as she wrote her tract.

Before they reached Calais to sail for England, she finished her manuscript, which Mr. Bracebridge proofed before sending it off to be printed. How accomplished Flo felt. And yet on August 21, 1850, she had to return to "busy idleness" herself. When she strolled into the drawing room at Lea Hurst, Mama and Parthe were stunned to see her. She introduced them to her owl, Athena. Mama's eyes grew more concerned by the moment as Flo's few belongings—mostly books—were set in the entry by the coachman.

"We outfitted you like a princess before you left," gasped Mama. "Where are all your fineries?"

"My dresses? My linens?" mulled Flo. "Why they are in Egypt and Greece and Germany. . . ."

"I do believe Flo has nothing left but the dress she's wearing," sputtered Parthe.

"I had to have something to wear," apologized Flo.

England seemed grim now. Of Flo's confidantes, only Aunt Mai was available. The entire family was jolted by the news that Henry Nicholson had drowned in Spain. Flo went to Waverly to console the family. In her heart, she did not pity Henry. Could one believe the words of Christ and pity those who had died? Death was a door to the Kingdom of God. But in consoling others, Flo's spirits sank to the depths again. Why was she alive? Her great plans were forever thwarted. The very day 1850 ended, she wrote her pain into a journal:

I have no desire now but to die. There is not a night that I do not lie down in my bed wishing that I may leave it no more. Unconsciousness is all that I desire. I remain in bed as long as I can, for what have I to wake for? I am perishing for want of food, and what prospect have I of better? While I am in this position, I can expect nothing else. Therefore, I spend my days in dreams of other situations which will afford me good. Alas, I now do little else.[10]

Seeing Richard Monckton Milnes at parties only depressed her more. He was cordial but cool. What had she expected? Did she actually want to encourage him? Hadn't she put him through enough torment? How could she be so selfish, so foolish? And yet his apparent indifference to her now stung like a whip. She also saw the extraordinary Elizabeth Blackwell again. Blackwell had returned from studying obstetrics in Paris. In the process, she had contracted an eye disease that cost her the sight of one eye. But her sacrifices had paid off. She was an eminently qualified doctor now, even if she would have to go back to America to practice medicine.

It seemed as though everyone Flo saw these days reminded her of her own failure. And her home life was more contentious than ever. Mama was exasperated with her. When was Flo going to outgrow these childish desires! Now Parthe joined Mama in being constantly irritated by Flo. On January 7, 1851, Flo wrote in her journal:

What is to become of me? . . . I can hardly open my mouth without giving dear Parthe vexation— everything I say or do is a subject of annoyance to her. And I, "Oh, how am I to get through this day?" is the thought of every morning, "How am I to talk through all this day?" And now, I feel as if I should not have strength ever to do anything else. My God, I love Thee, I do indeed. I do not say it in open rebellion, but in anguish and utter hopelessness, why didst Thou make me what I am? . . . It is not the unhappiness I mind, it is not indeed; but people can't be unhappy

Overcome by guilt, Flo tried to list all the good qualities of her family. Papa was a man of "good impulses." Mama was a "genius of order, to make a Place, to organize a parish, to form [by] her own exertions the best society in England." Parthe was "a child playing in God's garden and delighting in the happiness of all His works."[12]

"And what am I but a murderer among them, disturbing their happinesses?" she muttered.[13]

Flo began to write a very long tract of her unhappiness, her own restlessness. Perhaps that would give her insight, perhaps justification, or if nothing else, relief in something to do. Her tract grew into a treatise on activism. She talked to the Chartists, to Lord Ashley. Yes, the working people needed all the voices they could find among the aristocracy. England certainly had problems, not unsolvable at all but simply ignored by all the powers but a few. So Flo poured her heart into her tract. She discovered many working men angry with God, and quite a number refused to believe there was a God. Flo felt she had to straighten them out on this. Her tract changed direction. It grew into a treatise on theology.

Flo believed with all her heart that God was benevolent and His very thoughts were expressed as immutable physical laws. These physical laws that the atheistic materialists so cherished were evidence to Flo of His being. Flo even corresponded with a Catholic priest, hinting she might be more suited to Catholicism than Protestantism. But the priest saw that her chief attraction to Catholicism was the freedom of the sisters to nurse in clean, well-run hospitals. So he bluntly wrote her that her beliefs were not compatible with Catholicism.

Flo's relationship with Parthe worsened. Now Parthe was scheming with Mama to prick Flo's conscience and make her feel obligated to care for Grandmama Shore and all other aging relatives. The same technique had been used to divert Aunt Julia from becoming too active. Meanwhile, Parthe's health was getting worse, in no small part due to having a very difficult younger sister, Flo was told. Word that Richard Monckton Milnes was going to marry Annabel Crewe ignited Mama and Parthe for a while too. "How foolish Flo has been!" they ranted. This type of foolishness only made Parthe's health worse, said Mama. Finally Mama decided she should take Parthe to Karlsbad for bath treatments. Of course, Flo had to go too.

Once in Germany, Flo announced, "I'm going to Kaiserswerth while Parthe gets her treatments."

"What injustice!" screamed Parthe. "Flo ruins my health so that I have to come to Karlsbad. And while I'm here, she will go to Kaiserswerth!"

With that, Parthe hurled some jewelry into Flo's face. Mama was shocked. No one must know of this disgrace. Flo agreed to silence, but she did go to Kaiserswerth. Papa had not gone to Europe at all with the three. He was not supporting Flo yet, but he no longer supported Mama and Parthe against Flo. No less than the Bracebridges, the Bunsens, Aunt Mai, and the Sidney Herberts had recently urged Flo to break away from Mama and Parthe—if Papa didn't object. But Flo could not bring herself to make an open break. She had no financial support.

Still, Flo managed to return to Kaiserswerth. This time she worked with the deaconesses as an apprentice. Rising at five in the morning, she was consciously happy every waking moment until she fell asleep at night, exhausted. Four times during the day she was allowed ten minutes to eat: rye tea and bread at 6:00 a.m. and 3:00 p.m., broth and vegetables at noon, and broth only at 7:00 p.m. She would have been unhappy with more. It was weeks later, in October 1851, that she rejoined Mama and Parthe. Their resentment was smoldering. How dare Flo defy them?

Then, back in England, Flo was once again under their oppression. On her thirty-second birthday, she wrote to Papa:

> *I am glad to think that my youth is past & rejoice that it never can return, that time of follies & of bondage, of unfulfilled hopes & disappointed inexperience. . . . I am glad to have lived, though it has been a life which, except as the necessary preparation for another, few would accept. I hope now that I have come into possession of myself. I hope that I have escaped from that bondage. . . . I hope that I may live, a thing which I have not often been able to say, because I think I have learnt something which it would be a pity to waste.*[14]

Battling depression and frustration, she wrote *Cassandra*, a plaintive yet very angry eight-thousand-word essay on the frustrations of an English woman, married or unmarried. Among its many bitter complaints, she included:

> *Why have women passion, intellect, moral activity*

—these three—and a place in society where no one of the three can be exercised?

. . .Women are never supposed to have any occupation of sufficient importance not to be interrupted.

. . .Women long for an education to teach them to teach, to teach them the laws of the human mind and how to apply them.

. . .Dreaming always—never accomplishing; thus women live—too much ashamed of their dreams, which they think "romantic," to tell them where they will be laughed at.

. . .The chances are a thousand to one that, in that small sphere, the task for which that immortal spirit is destined by the qualities and the gifts which its Creator has placed within it, will not be found.

. . .This system dooms some minds to incurable infancy, others to silent misery.

. . .In a few rare, very rare cases. . .always provided in novels, but seldom to be met with in real life. . . [marriages] give food and space for the development of character and mutual sympathies.

. . .Jesus Christ raised women above the condition of mere slaves, mere ministers to the passions of the man, raised them by His sympathy. . . . [Yet] if anyone attempts the real imitation of Him, there are no bounds to the outcry with which the presumption of that person is condemned.

. . .To God alone may women complain without insulting Him!

. . .[The dying woman cries], "Free-free-oh! divine

freedom, art thou come at last? Welcome, beautiful death!"

...Give us back our suffering, we cry to Heaven in our hearts—suffering rather than indifferentism; for out of nothing comes nothing. But out of suffering may come the cure. Better have pain than paralysis! A hundred struggle and drown in the breakers. One discovers the new world. But rather, ten times rather, die in the surf, heralding the way to that new world, than stand idly on the shore![15]

In spite of her unhappiness, Flo now socialized within a very distinguished circle that included the Sidney Herberts, Lord Byron's wife, Elizabeth Barrett Browning, George Eliot, Lord Ashley, William Thackeray, Lord Palmerston, and poet Arthur Hugh Clough. They all acknowledged her insight into medicine and nursing. Yet all her efforts to participate in nursing orders were furiously opposed by Mama and Parthe. Still, Papa was finally stirring, waking up to her dilemma. But would he oppose Mama? Flo could not remember his ever doing that. Flo's only hope might be Parthe's illness, feigned or not. None other than Sir James Clark, the private physician to Queen Victoria, examined Parthe. His diagnosis: Parthe must be separated from Flo because her presence aggravated Parthe's delicate condition!

"Praise God!" sighed Flo for the irony.

Could Parthe argue with the distinguished Sir James Clark's diagnosis? Could Mama argue with it? Yes. They remained stubborn. Either Parthe's fits or the fancy that only Flo could nurse some sick relative nearly always managed to foil Flo's plans to visit medical facilities. In early 1853, at Tapton, Flo nursed Grandmama Shore—now ninety-five—through her final days. She felt the dear old lady's pulse die out. All the elderly relatives were now dead, and Mama herself was now sixty-five. Surely she would not hesitate to use her own old age to enslave Flo.

The time had come for Flo. She was almost thirty-three. Her resolve must be solid steel. No longer must she allow any excuse to deter her if an opportunity came.

ELEVEN

In the spring of 1853, Flo's opportunity came.

A group of wealthy aristocratic ladies wanted to create a medical facility: the Institute for the Care of Sick Gentlewomen. Elizabeth Herbert recommended Flo to manage it. On April 18, Flo was interviewed by Lady Canning. Flo backed up her reputation for nursing know-how with calm, articulate answers. Lady Canning seemed awed by the authority in Flo's manner. She could not hide her approval. But she was stunned when Flo set conditions to her acceptance.

"Gentlewomen of all religions must be accepted, not just members of the Church of England," insisted Flo.

Lady Canning presented Flo's demand to the Ladies' Committee. They accepted her terms. But Flo had not extended her conditions as far as she wanted. The institute would not care for poor women. The number of gentlewomen the institute could treat would not be great. Worst of all, Flo detected little enthusiasm in the Ladies' Committee for launching a nursing school. But still the opportunity was great.

Mama did not agree. "How can you think to degrade yourself so?" she stormed.

But that fury was nothing compared to the maelstrom Mama and Parthe raised when they discovered Papa had endowed Flo with a generous annual allowance! And he insisted they accept Flo's decision to head Lady Canning's institute. At last Papa had backed Flo, but the turmoil was so intense in Embley Park that Papa moved to London until things simmered down. Flo was elated. Surely now Mama and Parthe would stop interfering. But she was wrong. The two women worked relentlessly to modify Flo's plans. Why couldn't she start a nursing home near Embley Park?

"That way you can still live at home," meddled Mama.

Flo refused to negotiate. She moved to lodgings in London and planned the institute with the Ladies' Committee. They inspected houses on Upper Harley Street off Regent's Park. Flo knew exactly what she wanted: available hot water, quarters for nurses, and space to accommodate medical necessities. She found one building that was acceptable for a start. She went to Paris to study the medical facilities of the Sisters of St. Vincent, firing back by letter renovations to the Harley Street building. By August 1853, Flo had returned to open the institute, choosing to ignore the continued protests of Mama and Parthe. In the past, she had always answered them out of guilt—but no longer.

"I have far too much to do," she insisted.

But even Clarkey urged, "Won't you reconcile?"

"I have not taken this step, Clarkey dear," wrote Flo, "without years of anxious consideration. I mean the step of leaving them...[so] don't let us talk any more about this."[1]

Flo's will was hard-forged steel now. Her operation at Harley Street was very sophisticated for its time. Hot water was piped to every floor. Flo had determined it was most efficient to have the water heater on the top floor. Food and all medical supplies were lifted by a windlass to each floor—as well as the patients! "The nurse must not be a pair of legs for running up and down stairs," insisted Flo. In fact, the nurse should not leave her floor at all. She would have sleeping quarters on her floor. Patients could "ring" the nurse by means of a pull rope.

Flo immersed herself completely in the activity. There was no lack of immediate patients. She assisted a surgeon who removed a cancer then supervised the patient's recuperation. They used a new anesthetic called chloroform, recently pioneered by a physician named James Simpson. She nursed women with consumption. She consoled women suffering from hysteria. It was the compassionate but steely Flo who had to tell a woman she must surrender her bed if she appeared to be malingering. Flo nursed, she comforted, she inspired—as well as administered. She ordered and scavenged for furniture. She installed shelves. She kept accounts and inventoried. To Papa she confided how she managed the committee that was supposed to manage her!

When I entered into service here, I determined that, happen what would, I never would intrigue among the Committee. Now I perceive that I do all my business by intrigue. I propose in private to A, B, or C the resolution I think A, B, or C most capable of carrying in Committee, & then leave it to them—& I always win. I am now in the heyday of my power. Lady Cranworth, who was my greatest enemy, is now, I understand, trumpeting my fame through London.[2]

The institute thrived. The patients wrote her adoring, even loving, notes of thanks. Within a year, Flo had cut the cost of care for each patient by one-half! In the summer of 1854, cholera broke out in London, especially around the notorious slum area of St. Giles. Flo threw herself into the nursing effort, spending her time at Middlesex Hospital. She was committed to helping the sick, no matter how dangerous it was to herself. Her will—which she considered God's will—crushed objections raised by doctors. She did not influence by strident bullying, but calm reason and charm—and intrigue if necessary. She could tell that doctors who were meeting her for the first time expected a burly hellcat. She saw them blink in disbelief as they realized this thin, demure woman in front of them was Florence Nightingale. Then they fell under her spell. Her reputation grew. London had so many problems, she could stay feverishly busy there the rest of her life.

"But who could have predicted the events of late 1854?" she murmured.

In March 1854, England and France declared war on Russia. Because the notorious Russian czar, Nicholas, was expanding his empire south into Turkey, the English believed that the route to their precious crown jewel, India, was threatened. England had certainly won its share of wars, so the public reacted enthusiastically. The horror of war had been forgotten; after all, it had been thirty-nine years since Waterloo. In September the allies invaded the Crimea, an area of Russia on the Black Sea. At Sebastopol in Crimea, the Russians harbored their fleet. A direct attack on Sebastopol was deemed impossible, so the allies landed sixty-five thousand soldiers many miles north at the River Alma. But Russian forces, numbering forty thousand men and two hundred cannons, were there too.

"Still, we beat the Russian blighters at the Alma," announced Papa to Flo at Lea Hurst in October. "The backward Russians are still using muskets. Our men have rifles."

"How many good, decent men were lost?" sighed Flo.

"Hmm, a few thousand killed and wounded," he answered with less enthusiasm.

Flo, resting up from the London cholera siege, was somewhat distracted from the Crimean tragedy by a toothache and the presence at Lea Hurst of Susan Gaskell. Mrs. Gaskell was an accomplished writer who was writing a biography on the brilliant Charlotte Brontë. Flo had read Miss Brontë's advanced novels, written under the name Currer Bell, and wanted to know more about her. Instead, she found Mrs. Gaskell was burning with curiosity about *her*. In fact, the writer appeared in awe.

To a friend, Mrs. Gaskell wrote of Flo:

She is tall; very slight and willowy in figure; thick, shortish, rich brown hair; very delicate complexion; grey eyes, which are generally pensive and drooping, but when they choose can be the merriest eyes I ever saw; and perfect teeth, making her smile the sweetest I ever saw. Put a long piece of soft net and tie it round this beautifully shaped head. . . and dress her up in black silk high up to the long, white, round throat, and with a black shawl on—and you may get near an idea of her perfect grace and lovely appearance.

But this interesting domestic situation at Lea Hurst was trumped by developments stemming from the Crimean War.

In October, the *London Times* newspaper revealed that it had a reporter on the scene in Crimea. It was the first time ever for such civilian reporting. William Russell's reports were stinging too. By October 9, he was alerting all England to the horrible realities of war:

> *No sufficient preparations have been made for the care of the wounded. Not only are there not sufficient surgeons...not only are there no dressers and nurses...there are not even linens to make bandages.... Can it be said that the battle of the Alma has been an event to take the world by surprise? Yet...there is no preparation for the commonest surgical operations! Not only are the men kept, in some cases for a week, without the hand of a medical man coming near the wounds...but...the commonest appliances of the workhouse sick ward are wanting, and...the men must die through the medical staff of the British Army having forgotten that old rags are necessary for the dressing of wounds.*[3]

"So!" sputtered Papa. "We send off our magnificent Coldstream Guards, not to die from battle but from neglect!"

Mama noticed Flo preparing to leave. "You aren't leaving Lea Hurst, are you? I thought you had a bad toothache."

"I must be off to London."

Flo had received an offer from Lady Forester to finance a mission of mercy to the Crimean conflict. The British wounded were being brought back to Turkey, specifically to a suburb of Constantinople called Scutari. It was far from the combat area, so nurses would surely be accepted there. Flo left for London without hesitation. Besides the obvious need to go, the scathing criticism of the British army fell directly on Flo's good friends. Lord Palmerston was Home Secretary for Prime Minister Lord Aberdeen. But most affected was Sidney Herbert. He was the secretary of war. In London, Flo used her considerable influence with Lord Palmerston. Within hours, it seemed every powerful lord in the government was clearing a path for Flo's mission of mercy to the Crimea. By the time William Russell reported in the *Times* that the French wounded were very well served by the Sisters of Charity—and the editorial in the *Times* screamed, "Why have we no Sisters of Charity?"—Flo had her expedition of mercy organized!

On October 14, Flo wrote Elizabeth Herbert:

> *A small private expedition of nurses has been organized for Scutari & I have been asked to command it. . . . I do believe we may be of use.*[4]

Flo's letter crossed a letter in the mail from Sidney Herbert. On October 15, she read his appeal to her to take a group of nurses to the Crimea:

> *There is but one person in England that I know of who would be capable of organizing and superintending such a scheme. . . . Would you listen to the request to go and superintend the whole thing? . . . Deriving your authority from the Government, your position would secure the respect and consideration of everyone. . . together with a*

complete submission to your orders. I know these things
are a matter of indifference to you, except so far as they
may further the great objects you have in view.[5]

Herbert was angered and perplexed. He had been reassured by the chief medical officers in the Crimea that the facilities were excellent. What was going on? Flo gladly accepted the government endorsement. But as calm as any Duke of Wellington, Flo had already recruited thirty-eight nurses, including ten Catholic nuns, ordered uniforms made, arranged travel, and garnered medical supplies. Even the sudden arrival of Mama and Parthe, ecstatic at her sensation, did not rattle her. But their bad news did. Her owl, Athena, forgotten in all the excitement, had died of starvation.

"The poor little beastie," gasped Flo, bursting into tears.[6]

That was Flo's most traumatic moment in all the hectic preparation. Just six days after her letter from Sidney Herbert, Flo embarked with her contingent as "Superintendent of the female nursing establishment in the English General Military Hospitals in Turkey." Uncle Sam was to go with her as far as Marseilles. The Bracebridges agreed to accompany her all the way to Turkey. What colossal friends she had! The party crossed France by rail. Flo was very attentive to her nurses. She ate with them and pampered them. She promised new warm shoes at Marseilles.

Some nurses were astonished. "We ain't never had such attention before. It ain't the way of most genteel people with us."

In Marseilles, Flo loaded up on more supplies, in spite of the assurance of government authorities that it was not necessary. Before she boarded ship again on October 27, she was being heralded as a heroine—both in Britain and in France. Crowds gathered to cheer her. How could she ever justify such recognition? Then she learned that the *Times* had started a fund for her mission and had already raised a small fortune!

Not all her volunteers were happy. One nurse complained, "I came out prepared to submit to everything, to be put upon in every way. But there are some things, ma'am, one can't submit to. And if I'd known, ma'am, about the caps, great as was my desire to come out as nurse at Scutari, I wouldn't have come, ma'am."[7]

Flo was amused. The cap was very homely. Indeed the whole uniform was homely. By design. She wanted nothing to make the nurses attractive to the men. Frumpy. Frumpy. Frumpy. Her nurses wore a gray tweed dress, a gray worsted jacket, and a short woolen cape. Drab, drab, drab. Over the shoulders was a white Holland scarf and on the head a white cap. The cap was regarded by one and all as the ugliest of the ugly.

While crossing the Mediterranean on the *Vectis*, Flo learned more about the battle operations. The commander in chief of the British forces was Lord Raglan. Raglan was sixty-six and had lost an arm at the Battle of Waterloo many years before. The gore that awaited her was foreshadowed in a story she was told about Lord Raglan. After his arm was amputated at Waterloo, he yelled at an overeager assistant, "I say, don't throw that arm away just yet! One of the fingers has a ring my wife gave me."

Lord Raglan delegated authority to his field commanders. Queen Victoria's cousin, His Royal Highness the Duke of Cambridge, commanded a five-thousand-man division that included the highly publicized Coldstream Guards, Black Watch, and other elite units. Sir George Brown also commanded a division of five thousand-foot soldiers, as did Sir George De Lacy Evans. Cavalry, under Lord Lucan, consisted of the Light Brigade and the Heavy Brigade. Two additional divisions of foot soldiers were held in reserve.

Flo felt like she was already in battle. The *Vectis* fought storms so severe while crossing the Mediterranean that the cannons aboard had to be jettisoned. But finally on November 4, 1854, the ship anchored off Seraglio Point in the Bosporus, a strait that connected the Mediterranean Sea with the Black Sea. The day was grayed by falling rain. To the west sprawled Constantinople, thoroughly Muslim with its domes and minarets. To the east was Scutari, where the General Hospital and its enormous neighbor of blond brick, Barrack Hospital, sat conspicuously on a hill. According to Sidney Herbert's charge, the nursing in these two hospitals fell into Flo's jurisdiction. The two hospitals were supposed to care for up to three thousand wounded soldiers.

"Another nearby hospital that treats British officers is not included in my charge," she commented wistfully.

Coming aboard the *Vectis* to greet her was Lord Napier, representing Lord Stratford, the British ambassador to Turkey. Lord Stratford had "reigned" at Constantinople for sixteen years. His residence was virtually a palace, with twenty-five servants. He did not have a good reputation among the well-to-do in England. Some of the nicer things said about him were that he was "lazy, coldhearted, arrogant, and nasty-tempered." Certainly, Flo had not expected the sixty-eight-year-old potentate to greet her personally. And she suspected he would be of little help to her, whether she had powerful friends or not.

After a few pleasantries, Lord Napier's face clouded. "We had another great battle on October 25. The 'Battle of Balaclava' they are calling it. The ships will be bringing the wounded here in a few days."

Flo and her contingent were rowed ashore in the small, local *caiques*. The sight that greeted them was from hell. The bloated carcass of a horse lay rotting near the dock. Dogs fought each other as they ripped at the reeking flesh. A few soldiers loitered around the rickety wooden dock, undisturbed by the carnage. Wounded soldiers—unassisted—were struggling up the hill toward the hospitals. The hill was a quagmire of mud and garbage. Flo immediately determined that the dock was inadequate for receiving wounded from ships. And bringing them ashore in *caiques* in rough weather would only worsen their condition.

"I pray the hospital will not be so backward," she said grimly.

As Flo neared the Barrack Hospital with her nurses, it loomed up into its true immensity. It was no ancient palace, but the relinquished barracks of the Turkish army. Watchtowers stretched skyward from each corner of the three-storied quadrangle. Someone had said there were several miles of usable corridors inside, despite one entire side having been gutted by fire, and rumor had it that deep in its basements a small town of "camp followers" remained: hundreds of wives, prostitutes, and children.

Flo and the others entered Barrack Hospital through a massive gate. They were greeted by the chief medical officer, Dr. Menzies, and the military commandant, Major Sillery. Every impression after their cordial welcome was unfavorable. The floors in the corridors had loose tiles. The walls ran damp. Flo's contingent was allotted five cramped rooms. One served Flo as her office, although it doubled as Mr. Bracebridge's bedroom. Another of the five rooms was still occupied by the decaying corpse of a Russian general! Furniture was almost nonexistent in every room and corridor. Trash was scattered everywhere. The central yard of the quadrangle was a virtual dump. Rats darted in and out of the refuse.

"You will receive a daily ration of one pint of water per person," advised Dr. Menzies. "I'm terribly sorry there are no cooking facilities for you."

"We'll manage," said Flo, hiding her shock.

How were the wounded being fed? Her search led to a dirty kitchen with thirteen five-gallon copper pots. These pots had to feed more than two thousand men! The cooking techniques were barbaric. Food was prepared by soldiers, not chefs. Chunks of crudely butchered animals were thrown into water that often was not even hot enough to simmer. Vegetables were nowhere to be seen. Eventually the "broth" was served in bowls. The patients had no other utensils. The army assumed they had utensils with their mess kits, but of course the wounded rarely had more than the clothes on their backs. Ironically, no spoon or fork was necessary, because the bowl rarely contained any meat but the smallest scrap.

"This meat-flavored water is the sum total of a patient's diet!" Flo realized with horror.

As for special rations for those who could not take this broth, they didn't exist. There was no organization to handle such a request. On the other hand, Flo discovered that in most matters the army was bogged down in bureaucracy. Over several decades of peace, the army had implemented hundreds of checks and counterchecks to cut spending. Now they were choking on these precautions. Every request proceeded at a snail's pace. Requisitions needed the signature of two doctors. Then the purveyor processed it, passing it on to the commissariat, who was supposed to negotiate contracts for the purchase.

"Our noses make us painfully aware of another major problem here," Flo told Sig, without a trace of humor in her voice.

The hospital operation had a monstrous—possibly deadly—problem, which manifested itself immediately by assaulting the nose. The pervading smell was that of a crowded barnyard on the hottest day. Flo soon discovered that the great building had abominable sewers, which often backed up, spewing human waste out into the wards. To counteract this unspeakable filth, the doctors had started the use of huge chamber pots. One chamber pot served about fifty men. Flo learned that the reeking pots stood unemptied for days at a time.

Then Flo saw the wounded. It was another ghastly scene from hell.

TWELVE

Could hell be worse than this? Flo asked herself.

She had seen much sickness—yes, even death — in her life, but not of this magnitude, not of this unimaginable gore. Most of the British soldiers were ripped, torn, and mutilated. Arms, legs, eyes, noses, ears, jaws were gone, replaced by filthy, blood-clotted rags! Flo had to fight tears of sympathy, then of rage. All but a few of the wounded men sprawled on the broken tile floors. There were few beds, few blankets. No hospital garb was issued, although supposedly hundreds of outfits had been sent from England. No one knew where the outfits were. The men lay in their rotting battle gear, infested head to toe with lice. One doctor had implemented a routine for bathing the men. But it processed only thirty men a day!

"A patient is washed once in eighty days," calculated Flo, almost numb from shock.

But then she noted that one sponge was used for all thirty men. No wonder the hospital was rife with cholera, lice, and fleas. Perhaps it was a blessing *not* to be washed. Well, she and her nurses could change that.

Then Dr. Menzies floored Flo. "The doctors are under orders to allow you to quarter here. But you must not assist them unless they specifically request it."

Flo bit her tongue. She must not label this revelation as the monumental stupidity it was. She had always found biblical wisdom best, and Proverbs 29:11 advised, *"A fool uttereth all his mind: but a wise man keepeth it in till after-wards."* But this shock was as great as any she had suffered. Still, she could keep her nurses occupied for some time making slings, pillows, mattresses, anything to help the wounded. Even a stubborn doctor would use those things if they were lying about available.

Over the next few days, Flo and her contingent settled in. The doctors did indeed resist true nursing care offered by Flo and her nurses. Flo wasted no time, though, procuring vegetables and meat from the local markets with the large fund she had available. With the portable stoves she had brought, her nurses prepared food and managed to dispense it. The doctors didn't object. Perhaps they didn't notice.

"I've received the most distressing news about the Battle of Balaclava," confided Charles Bracebridge.

The Russians had sprung a surprise attack on the British naval base at Balaclava, a mere seven miles from the main Russian naval base at Sebastopol. If the Russians would have captured the supply ships, what a masterstroke that would have been. Only 550 Highlanders, under Colin Campbell, and fewer than twelve hundred British cavalry were there to defend the base. The forces opposed each other in the floor of a valley. The British reacted quickly, sending a division of five thousand foot soldiers to join the fray. But they soon learned the Russian force numbered thirty thousand! Nevertheless, the Russian offensive stalled, intimidated by the fierce fighting they encountered. Eventually, however, they began to move forward again, exposing four thousand of their cavalry. Opposing them was the five-hundred-man cavalry of General Scarlett's Heavy Brigade. The Heavy Brigade charged viciously. Although much greater in strength, the Russians seemed stunned. Their cavalry were thrown into chaos. The moment was perfect for the British Light Brigade to attack and hammer the Russians. An order arrived for the Light Brigade to attack.

"But Lord Cardigan refused," Charles Bracebridge told Flo.

His refusal was not incomprehensible. He had been promised infantry support. The five-thousand-man division had not yet arrived. Another order reached him: "Attack immediately." But by now the situation had changed. The Russians had mustered a battery of twelve cannons at their end of the valley. With the heavy guns were three thousand reorganized Russian cavalry troops. Russian infantry lined both flanks of the valley. Lord Cardigan again questioned the order to attack. His superior, Lord Lucan, ordered him to advance. Lord Cardigan, riding ahead of his ranks, advanced his 663 cavalry down the valley in a trot. They were fired on from three sides. They came within eighty yards of the cannons, but could advance no farther against the withering fire. Only seventy members of the Light Brigade managed to return unscathed to the main British lines; another 125 limped back wounded. Nearly five hundred were dead. The Light Brigade had been almost annihilated when, incredibly, the Russians stopped their attack. Almost as amazing, Lord Cardigan survived, dining that night on his yacht in the harbor.

A French officer who had witnessed the courageous "Charge of the Light Brigade" said sadly, "It's magnificent—but it's not war."

Of course, there were far more British casualties than those of the Light Brigade. After already suffering for two weeks, the wounded from the battle began to arrive by ship at Scutari. To compound the problem, another battle took place at Inkerman on November 5. These wounded also were headed for Scutari. Russian wounded were brought to the hospital too. The resistance of the doctors against Flo and her nurses evaporated under the onslaught of suffering. Flo wrote a doctor friend in London about events of November 9:

> *On Thursday last, we had 1,715 sick and wounded in this Hospital (among whom were 120 cholera patients) and 650 severely wounded in the other building, called the General Hospital, of which we also have charge, when a message came to me to prepare for 510 wounded on our side of the Hospital, who were arriving from the dreadful affair. . . at Balaclava, where were 1,763 wounded and 442 killed besides 96 officers wounded and 38 killed. . . . We had but half an hour's notice before they began landing the wounded. Between one and nine o'clock, we had the mattresses stuffed, sewn up, and laid down. . .the men washed and put to bed, and all their wounds dressed . . . . Twenty-four cases [died] on the day of landing. We now have four miles of beds, and not eighteen inches apart. . . . As I went my night-rounds among the newly-wounded that night, there was not one murmur, not one groan. . . . These poor fellows bear*

pain and mutilation with an unshrinking heroism
which is really superhuman, and die, or are cut up
without a complaint. . . . We have all the sick cookery
now to do—and I have got in four men for the
purpose. . . . I hope in a few days we shall establish a
little cleanliness. But we have not a basin, nor a towel,
not a bit of soap, not a broom. I have ordered three
hundred scrubbing brushes.[1]

The patients in both hospitals almost doubled to nearly four thousand. The surgical operations began immediately:

One poor fellow, exhausted with hemorrhage, has his
leg amputated as a last hope, and dies ten minutes after
the surgeon has left him. Almost before the breath has
left his body, it is sewn up in a blanket and carried
away and buried the same day. We have no room for
corpses in the wards.[2]

The hospital was so poorly supplied that the surgeons had neither screens nor tables. Flo ordered these things out of her private fund. Instead of pleasing the doctors, this gesture irritated them. Why did she have such resources when they had almost none? Flo chose to be hopeful about the medical staff:

We are very lucky in our Medical Heads. Two of them are
brutes and four are angels—for this work which makes
either angels or devils of men and women, too. As for the
assistants, they are all Cubs. . . . But unlicked Cubs grow

up into good old Bears, though I don't know how.[3]

She appealed to Sidney Herbert to send supplies by comparing the abysmal facilities of British hospitals with the comparatively lavish facilities of the French hospitals. Nothing could make a British politician react more vigorously than that. To be outdone by the French, indeed! If events were not already grim enough for the British army, the Crimea was hammered by a hurricane on November 14. Tents and supplies were whipped into the frozen hinterlands by the wind. The *Prince,* which carried winter clothing and supplies for the British troops, sank in Balaclava harbor. So the soldiers were exposed to the elements with no winter gear. Temperatures in Constantinople and Scutari dropped below freezing many nights from December through February. Snow was common. The Crimea was even colder.

"Blasted luck," gasped Charles Bracebridge in a choked voice. "The British army is being destroyed!"

When Flo's family wrote to tell her of all the praise she was receiving in England, she protested, "Praise good God! He knows what a situation He has put upon me. For His sake, I bear it willingly, but not for the sake of Praise. The cup which my Father hath given me, shall I not drink it?"[4] In spite of all her past metaphysical cogitation, she always lapsed into orthodox Christianity for comfort in the grim present and for hope in the uncertain future.

Meanwhile, Flo's request to Lord Stratford, the ambassador to Constantinople, for help at the hospital was answered by Lady Stratford. The fine lady was so appalled by the foulness of the hospital—she had visited it but once—she tried to pull Flo away to "help" her. Flo was forced to ask Sidney Herbert to politely beseech Lady Stratford to stop interfering, because the well-intentioned lady was a "time waster and impediment." Instead of bumbling interference, Flo told Herbert, her nurses—and the doctors—would be greatly helped by an expediter, a man who could cut through the maze of bureaucracy. Even without such assistance, by mid-December she was able to write Herbert that she had a kitchen set up to provide special diets for those patients who needed it. The wards were at long last being scrubbed by nurses. Both patients and gowns were being regularly washed by nurses. Wounds were dressed daily by nurses. Flo had charmed the assistants in the wards into emptying the chamber pots daily although it was a nauseating chore. She had bought out of her own funds six thousand hospital gowns, two thousand pairs of socks, and hundreds of nightcaps, slippers, plates, cups, and utensils. She hired two hundred Turkish workers, whom she personally directed, to restore the burned-out corridors. Soon those corridors would hold beds for another eight hundred wounded. Nor had she neglected the camp followers living in the basements. Many of these destitute women she employed as laundresses. Her chief complaint was of those who wouldn't work or who prevented others from working.

"These 'ungovernables' exhaust me," she admitted.

The situation soon worsened. Late in December, Flo heard that a group of nearly fifty women was arriving to help. They were completely unqualified. Flo was furious. Before she left England, she had specifically asked Sidney

Herbert not to send any more nurses until she requested them. She had his agreement in writing. All logic and common sense told Flo that a small number of very disciplined nurses was far better than a large number of undisciplined ones. Now she wrote Herbert an angry missive: "You have sacrificed your own written word to a popular cry. You must feel that I ought to resign." But she tempered her anger with, "I only remain till I have provided in some measure for these poor wanderers."

Soon the fifty newcomers inundated the hospital. Many were aristocratic ladies, more interested in meeting officers than in nursing. Flo loathed amateur nurses, ladies or not. Her pessimism was borne out. The new arrivals disrupted the order she had created in the hospital. They refused to answer to her. She tried to have the newcomers removed from the hospital. Flo's hostility toward the newcomers was seized upon by a few doctors who resented her power. And she had no friends in the purveyor and the commissariat, who considered her pure evil for circumventing their purchasing power. Then came betrayal. One of her own group sent a letter to the *London Times* condemning not only Flo's efforts but her arrogance. The use of nurses, which had appeared so promising, was falling apart.

Weary and depressed, she still wrote home with wit:

Such a tempest has been brewed in this little pint-pot as you could have no idea of. But, I like the [donkey], have put on the lion's skin, and when I have done that, (poor me, who never affronted any one before), I can bray so loud that I shall be heard, I am afraid, as far as

England. However this is no place for lions and as for [donkeys], we have enough.[5]

But if certain enemies thought Flo was in retreat, they could not have been more mistaken. To alleviate the overcrowding of "nurses," she sent ten of her own back to England, including, of course, the letter writer. Flo, who had always been intrigued by the way English servants made a great house run smoothly, next proceeded to take on the hospital bureaucracy. Earlier, she had called for an expediter for her own effort, but since then she had decided that the maze of regulations—indeed, the organization itself— had to be changed. The abysmal state of the hospital when she arrived proved the system did not work. The procedures and the organization were abominations, but none of the doctors or professional soldiers would champion changes.

"This 'disloyalty' could end their careers," she reasoned.

While she worked out a plan for reform, the wounded kept arriving. On January 2, a contingent of twelve hundred arrived! Besides being wounded and sick, nearly all suffered from scurvy. Lime juice had been sent to the soldiers to prevent this disease, but somehow it had been lost! On January 4, Flo wrote Sidney Herbert that properly executed requisitions to the purveyor at the hospital were nearly futile. Requested but out of stock were gowns, socks, underwear, plates, and drinking cups. The purveyor had only a handful of bedpans to satisfy the need for thousands. There was a shipment of twenty-seven thousand flannel gowns somewhere—but the purveyor did not know where!

By January 28, 1855, Flo was at last ready to take on the bureaucracy of army medical facilities. In her letter to Sidney Herbert, she first apologized for her very unpleasant role; she felt like a spy. But changes had to be made. As secretary of war, he had the power to make changes. She offered as an example of present inefficiency the purchase and distribution of fresh meat. Every morning, orderlies had to requisition rations for the day from the commissariat. Much meat—as precious as it was—spoiled in the delay. Flo recommended that every bed in a ward have a ticket identifying which diet its patient was on. Wardmasters, supervised by doctors, should requisition needed food the day before it was distributed. Meat should be sent directly to the kitchen. Also, every patient must have his own bed with all necessary bedding. If blankets or linens wore out, the wardmaster—a position Flo regarded as the equivalent of a hotel manager or head housekeeper—must requisition replacements. The wardmaster must also oversee the delivery of incoming patients, cooking, cleaning, and washing. Flo offered numerous other changes and cited examples.

To administer her changes, Flo recommended a "governor," one man instead of a disinterested—usually distant—committee as now. Because it was a military hospital, the governor should be an officer. Under the governor would be four officials: one for administering daily hospital routine, one for procuring food, one for procuring furniture and clothing, and one to be the medical head in charge of the doctors. Flo was diplomatic enough to praise certain enlightened individuals. But she knew well that her recommendations to Sidney Herbert would not be taken kindly by those currently in power at the hospital.

All she could do in the meantime was persist in her battle for progress at Scutari. She continued to chronicle the exasperating deficiencies:

> *We have lost the finest opportunity for advancement of the cause of medicine and erecting it into a science which will ever be afforded. Here there is no operating room, no dissecting room, post mortem examinations are seldom made and then in the dead-house, no statistics (the ablest staff surgeon here told me that he considered that he had killed hundreds of men owing to the absence of these) are kept as to what ages most deaths occur, as to modes of treatment, appearance of the body after death. . . [all the] most important points which contribute to making Therapeutics a means of saving life.*[6]

Flo had her supporters in England, including the queen. Sidney Herbert wrote Flo that Her Royal Majesty wished Miss Nightingale to tell the noble wounded and sick men that no one took a warmer interest in their recovery or admired their courage more than their Queen Victoria. And the queen wished Herbert to pass on frequently to her the accounts he received from Miss Nightingale. Flo had the chaplains read the queen's words to the men in the wards. But this raised another issue. Though encouraged, the men complained bitterly that the army had cut their pay when they were sick or wounded. Couldn't Queen Victoria do anything about it? Flo relayed their complaint.

Next, Flo learned that Londoners were warring over whether she was a force for good or for evil. She closed one letter by saying she had heard "a religious war about poor me"[7] was being carried on in the *Times*, and she was grateful that Elizabeth Herbert was one of her most enthusiastic defenders. Apparently the queen was too. Flo added, "God has given me such good friends."[8]

The English public was fussing over far more than Florence Nightingale. They were in a fury over the bungled conduct of the war. "Half the British army is dead or in hospital!" some screamed. Others speculated that Prime Minister Lord Aberdeen's government might fall. "Oh no!" agonized Flo. What if Sidney Herbert was replaced as secretary of war? Flo's entire effort might disintegrate. Who would support her demands for reform then? Which ladies—qualified by nothing more than friendships in the new government—would arrive to take over the "nursing" of the hospital?

To her horror, Lord Aberdeen's government did fall.

THIRTEEN

Lord Aberdeen was replaced by an almost blind, almost deaf man of seventy-one. The new prime minister was openly besmirched by the opposition as an old geezer with false teeth that would fall out of his mouth if he did not speak with such hesitation! Flo knew him well.

"The new prime minister is my neighbor and good friend Lord Palmerston!" celebrated Flo.

Instead of being a disaster, the new government appeared a colossal good fortune for Flo. She regretted losing Sidney Herbert, but with a sponsor like Lord Palmerston, Flo could work with Herbert's replacement, Lord Panmure. Then Flo heard of another change of government. The enemy's leader, Czar Nicholas, had died. Would his successor, Alexander II, be more likely to negotiate peace? Perhaps not. But Flo's optimism about the new British government was borne out. Her entreaties to all her powerful friends led to the formation of a Sanitary Commission. The driving force on the commission was Dr. John Sutherland. This team came to Scutari in early March of 1855.

Dr. Sutherland and his team were appalled by the Barrack Hospital. They judged the sewers murderous. The sewers were so vast and so clogged that the hospital seemed floating in filth. In addition, the water supply, meager though it was, had other problems. It was contaminated. The team found a dead horse in one conduit! They hired workers to flush and clean the sewers. Contaminants in the water supply were removed. All refuse was carried out, and the central yard was cleared. Rotting wood pallets found throughout the hospital were ripped out. Scavenging rats were exterminated. Walls, floors, and ceilings were washed with lime.

Another great contribution by Lord Panmure—or those back in London who influenced him—was the arrival of a master chef to run the kitchens at the hospitals. Alexis Soyer appeared a comic Frenchman, but he was not a gourmet cook. His forte was cooking enormous amounts of simple food that was both nutritious and appetizing. He baked bread. He made soups and stews. He trained soldiers to be cooks. He designed a camp stove for soldiers to cook with.

"Oh, how promising it all seems now," reflected Flo.

Her first four months at the hospital had been permanently etched in her memory. Misery and hope. Tragedy and triumph. Often she had been on her knees eight hours straight dressing wounds. She comforted men headed for surgery. She had a gift for calming them. Some soldiers called her the "Lady-in-Chief." Others called her the "lady with the lamp," because she carried a glowing lamp as she made seemingly never-ending rounds in the dark corridors. She personally had attended two thousand men on their deathbeds. She had been told by many of the officers that the common soldier was the scum of the earth. Now she knew the character of the common soldier was in many ways superior to that of the officers. She organized reading rooms. She urged the soldiers not to drink. They told her they drank because they couldn't send their money home. She resolved to change that when she had time. In the meantime, perhaps, she could hire a tutor to teach the illiterate soldiers to read and write.

"Absolutely not!" screamed one high-ranking officer. "Haven't you spoiled these brutes enough?"

But she went ahead anyway. She admired the common soldiers very much and considered them—just as the common village people in England were—victims of prejudice by the well-to-do. To those in England, she wrote:

What the horrors of war are, no one can imagine, they are not wounds and blood and fever, spotted and low, and dysentery chronic and acute, cold and heat and famine. They are intoxication, drunken brutality, demoralization and disorder on the part of the inferior—jealousy, meanness, indifference, selfish brutality on the part of the superior. . . . [The common soldiers] are much more respectful to me than they are to their own officers.[1]

In the same letter, she reemphasized she was "in sympathy with God, fulfilling the purpose I came into the world for."[2] She also warned, "Beware of Lady Stratford," whom she now considered not an artless bumbler but a sly, two-faced threat.[3] The lady must not be trusted with any confidence. Flo slept behind a screen in a storeroom. About the only responsibility she delegated was management of the "free gift" stores. These were stockpiles of gifts sent by the British people and entrusted to her to distribute to the soldiers. Sig Bracebridge did that chore for her. During the day—her body warmed by a black wool dress with white cuffs, and collar and head covered by a white cap under a black silk handkerchief—Flo nursed, supervised, requisitioned supplies, received callers, and wrote correspondence. Her writing was mountainous: records, reports, requisitions, letters for the men, letters for the nurses, and letters for herself. Often, in the wee hours, she would lurch from her writing desk onto her bed and pass out from exhaustion. Sig would wake her in the morning.

With good sanitation, good food, good nursing, and good morale added to good medical treatment, the mortality rate at the Barrack Hospital began to fall. When Flo first arrived, a man had an even chance he would die if admitted to the hospital! By the end of March, the mortality rate was 15 percent; by the end of April, it reached 10 percent and was still falling. Was her effort appreciated by Dr. Hall, the chief of medical staff of the British army? Not at all, she learned. He felt threatened. Flo wanted to visit the facilities in the Crimea itself, starting with the two hospitals at Balaclava, where Dr. Hall resided. Dr. Hall insisted she had no authority outside Turkey.

"But for the sake of the soldiers, I must go," she told Sig.

On May 5, 1855, she sailed on the *Robert Lowe* across the Black Sea to Balaclava. Alexis Soyer and Charles Bracebridge were in her party. Aboard ship, she wrote home of the irony of accompanying four hundred of her patients back to the front where they might be shot. Flo arrived in the Balaclava harbor, the main British naval base, with its vast thicket of masts on the ships, only to discover that Lord Raglan was elsewhere. Dr. Sutherland of the Sanitary Commission and John McNeill, representing a second commission investigating the supply protocol and performance of the British army, came to greet her.

Atop fine riding horses, the gentlemen took her out among the fortifications. The British army and its retinue in Balaclava numbered almost two hundred thousand. Tents were still used by many thousands of British soldiers, but wooden barracks were being added as rapidly as they could be built. The route was muddy.

"And the air foul," added the fastidious Soyer.

Flo shuddered to see men marching toward the trenches to watch for a Russian attack from Sebastopol, only seven miles away. Nevertheless, she characterized Balaclava as "the most flowery place you can imagine."[4] A sergeant presented her with a bouquet. She remembered him well. Flo had saved his life at Scutari, after noticing his inert form in the corridor during one of her nocturnal rounds. Thorough to the last, she had examined him under her lamp. Good gracious! The man had never been attended at all. Somehow he had been missed. He was beyond protesting. He was dying, helpless to make a sound. A bullet was in his eye! Praise God, she had found a surgeon, who saved him. And to imagine this same sergeant back on the front! Flo was astonished as more and more soldiers gathered around their small party. At first dozens, then hundreds, then thousands. They began to cheer. For her? Surely not. But for whom? They appeared to be gawking at her.

Alexis Soyer removed all doubt. "Behold the heroic daughter of England, the soldiers' friend!" he shouted.[5]

The soldiers cheered her until it was deafening. More bouquets of wildflowers were presented to her.

"Pick the best one," they clamored.

"I pick them all," she cried, hugging the flowers to her chest. The reception overwhelmed her. "Give God the praise," she tried to yell, but emotion choked her voice.

Her reception at the General Hospital the next day was as hostile as the previous one was loving. Not only was Dr. Hall cool, but the nurses were openly unfriendly.

"I should have sooner expected to see the queen here as you," said one nurse rudely.[6]

Flo discovered she was the victim of vicious rumors. According to her persecutors, she lived in luxury at Scutari with her own French chef. She plundered the free gifts intended for the soldiers. She was in every way aristocratic and arrogant. But Flo was unflappable. Never did she rise to the bait. She didn't acknowledge rude remarks but stolidly proceeded with her inspection. She went on to Castle Hospital, on the heights outside Balaclava. Both Castle Hospital and General Hospital were filthy and poorly administered, replicas of Scutari before Flo arrived. But the terrible inefficiencies seen here were the direct result of the iron hand of Dr. Hall. He prevented every measure for improvement. He made every requisition as difficult to fill as possible. It was then that Flo realized he was the one who had reassured Sidney Herbert in London the previous fall that the medical facilities for British soldiers were top drawer. But time and the British government were on her side. If the two commissions did their work in Balaclava, the truth would be known in London eventually. And she must do her work now. But her old enemy—disease—intervened.

"What happened?" said Flo, surprised to find herself

peering up into Charles Bracebridge's concerned face.

"You fainted."

"You have 'Crimea fever,' ma'am," said a doctor.

And fever seized her. Her last coherent thought was that the doctor was probably right. If this was the onset of cholera, she would have diarrhea. Oh, but this disease was bad enough. She writhed in a hospital bed against a consuming heat. Every bone ached. The medical staff tried to restrain her, but Flo was in a nightmare. She was delirious. She rose against their wishes. She scribbled madly at a desk. She imagined a Persian adventurer coming and getting a draft for three hundred thousand pounds sterling from Charles Bracebridge. Her notes were gibberish. One day, the doctors had to shave her head—anything to dissipate the heat. Slowly the maddening heat went away. Gradually she came to her senses. She had been in her nightmare for two weeks, her nurse said. Flo had no energy to write now. She could not even get out of bed. Her voice was a weak whisper.

On May 24, she heard her nurse say in exasperation, "Well, of course this is Miss Nightingale's room!" Flo heard a scuffle. The nurse gasped, "But you can't come in here!"

"My name is Raglan. Miss Nightingale knows me very well."[7]

It was Lord Raglan, commander in chief of all British forces! The old man didn't look much better than she felt. It was clear he was working himself to death. Nevertheless, he acted delighted to learn she was recovering. He was bubbling over with other good news too. The allies were moving again, at this very moment attacking the Strait of Kertch, through which Russian supply ships traveled. He had every reason to believe the assault would succeed.

He left her, saying, "I will telegraph Her Majesty that you are out of danger. She inquires about you constantly." He blinked around the room. "Good heavens, I have never seen so many flowers."

"The soldiers are so kind," answered Flo.

"The soldiers? Those brutes did this?"

Sig then arrived to help care for Flo. It was decided that Flo would be better off at Scutari. The medical staff of Balaclava arranged for her to be put aboard the *Jura*. But before it sailed, Charles Bracebridge discovered it was the one ship in the fleet that would not stop in Scutari. Once underway, it would go on to England! Hurriedly, Flo and her party transferred to another ship. Flo was utterly convinced the selection of the *Jura* by the medical staff of Balaclava was no accident. Dr. Hall was behind it. He still hadn't learned that Flo had direct lines to the very top of the British Empire!

At Scutari, she was installed in a house to convalesce. Dr. Sutherland told her, "That fever saved your life. You were most assuredly working yourself to death."

In June, Flo was dismayed to hear that Lord Raglan had died. The cause of death was officially deemed cholera, but Flo thought he had worked himself to death, just as she might have. Lord Raglan's replacement, the new commander in chief, took no note whatsoever of Flo. She was effectively being removed from any influence on the medical facilities in his theater of war. Apparently the new commander did not appreciate her lofty connections any more than did Dr. Hall. Yet she knew her work in the Crimea was far from done. Her suggestions for improving conditions at the Balaclava hospitals had not yet been implemented.

The next months—during which Flo visited Balaclava off and on—were very difficult. The Bracebridges—her greatest moral support—sailed back to England at the end of July. The woman Flo picked to replace Sig in running the free gift storehouse in Scutari turned out to be a thief. Her room and her assistants' rooms were bursting with stolen goods. Among the stolen free gifts were articles of Flo's own clothing! Sending the thief away meant Flo had to assume that burdensome duty again herself. When the doctors in both Scutari and Balaclava realized that Dr. Hall considered Flo a nuisance, their attitude toward her changed from cooperation to indifference to hostility. Still, she persisted.

In September, Aunt Mai arrived for a visit.

"Flo!" she gasped, visibly shocked by her niece's appearance.

The long, thick locks were gone. And Flo's trim figure was now cadaverous. Aunt Mai helped her as best she could. That same month, the British took the Russian stronghold at Sebastopol. The war was won, if not over. But Flo's fortunes were not so bright as the British army's. Back in England, the woman Flo had dismissed from the free gift storehouse was libeling Flo as the thief! Then, in a public meeting in October, Charles Bracebridge foolishly attacked the medical establishment of the British army—at the same time lauding Flo. If reporting by the *Times* was accurate, his charges were embarrassingly inexact. Many thought Flo was behind his attack. The medical staff in Scutari and Balaclava became even more hostile. Flo wrote to Bracebridge and urged him to be silent.

"His attacks only worsen my situation here," she fretted.

Despite the controversy, in November, Flo was feted in England. The Duke of Cambridge, a powerful royal and veteran of the Crimean War, chaired the occasion. Richard Monckton Milnes, Sidney Herbert, and others started a Florence Nightingale Fund. The fund was intended to help Flo establish a school of nursing after the war. Parthe and Mama were ecstatic in writing Flo about her exalted stature in England.

Then a brooch arrived for Flo in Scutari from Queen Victoria. Prince Albert had personally designed it for her. It was topped by three large diamonds, each the center of a star with five smaller diamonds. The border read "Blessed Are the Merciful." In the middle of a red cross in the center were a crown and the initials "VR." At the bottom of the brooch a banner declared "Crimea." On the reverse was etched "To Miss Florence Nightingale, as a mark of esteem and gratitude for her devotion towards the Queen's brave soldiers from Victoria R. 1855."[8]

The brooch is far too grand, Flo thought. But it presented her with a wonderful opportunity to write to the queen and her consort directly. Along with her thanks, she intended to champion the cause of the common soldier. As she had promised, Flo had already set up a system for sending the soldiers' pay home. She had to do it herself. The army had firmly rejected the idea at the same time they spurned her suggestion that a tutor be hired to teach the soldiers to read and write. In her own system, she kept meticulous records of the money, sending the combined sum of many soldiers' pay to Uncle Sam in England. He parceled out the money to the soldiers' families according to Flo's records. But why should the army itself not offer this convenience to its soldiers? Flo implored the queen to help with the problem. The lack of such a system for sending money home and the lack of schooling were leading contributors to the soldiers' heavy drinking.

"Every penny they send home is a penny they do not spend on alcohol!" she insisted. "And every minute they study in school is a minute they do not drink alcohol."

Lord Panmure objected that it was nonsense that a system was not in place for soldiers to send their pay home. But he found out he was wrong. And just as he had shown a willingness to send commissioners to investigate army practices, he showed a willingness to institute necessary changes. In the future, strategically located offices would be available to sell money orders to the soldiers. Thus they could safely send money home to their families.

Flo attended a Christmas party in Constantinople. She wore Queen Victoria's brooch on a black dress. Few noticed the jewelry, however, because they were stunned by the appearance of her face. She knew she must have looked very ill, with her hair not yet grown out. Her hair was virtually a man's haircut with bangs. She was so weak, she had to sit on a couch most of the evening. And she was so unused to gaiety that she found herself laughing hysterically at any anecdote.

In spite of her many triumphs, Flo felt a failure. The never-ending work—usually under great stress—was gnawing her nerves raw. Factions gossiped and schemed against her. She learned that the smiling Lady Stratford had assured one and all that Flo probably did steal from the free gift storehouse. She heard that Dr. Hall encouraged any report that fingered her for some misdemeanor.

Although the war ended February 28, 1856, the men maimed in battle still had to be cared for. Flo remained, though not at peace. In March, remembering the army's many blunders, Flo wrote, "I am in a state of chronic rage. . . ." And her outrage over the contempt the officers had for the common soldier festered. To Uncle Sam, she wrote:

I have never seen so teachable and helpful a class as the army [soldier] generally. Give them opportunity promptly and securely to send money home—and they will use it. Give them a school and a lecture and they will come to it. Give them a book and a game and a [slide show]. . .and they will leave off drinking. Give them suffering and they will bear it. Give them work and they will do it.[9]

In January 1856, John McNeill and Colonel Tulloch brought a report before Parliament. Slowly, it became apparent that the report was a bombshell, confirming everything Flo had written her friends and superiors in London. As if Dr. Hall and his colleagues had not been hammered hard enough by the report, in March they received the final blow. It seemed Lord Panmure had sent a man—Colonel Lefroy—to secretly investigate the situation in the Crimea. He was to check not only on the medical staff but also on

Flo. His report to Lord Panmure resulted in a general order to be posted in every barrack and every mess hall in the British army!

It appears to me that the Medical Authorities of the Army do not correctly comprehend Miss Nightingale's position as it has been officially recognized by me. I therefore think it right, to state to you briefly for their guidance, as well as for the information of the Army, what the position of this excellent lady is. Miss Nightingale is recognized by Her Majesty's Government as the General Superintendent of the Female Nursing Establishment of the military hospitals of the Army. No lady, or sister, or nurse, is to be transferred from one hospital to another, or introduced into any hospital without consultation with her. . . . The Principal Medical Officer will communicate with Miss Nightingale upon all subjects connected with the Female Nursing Establishment, and will give his directions through that lady.[10]

Flo's triumph for nursing in the Crimea was officially and utterly complete.

FOURTEEN

The British war machine in the Crimea was slowly disassembled. The sick and the wounded were the last to leave—along with the nurses. To one of her nurses, who was departing in April 1856, Flo revealed her true Christian feeling: "It matters little, provided we spend our lives to God, whether like our Blessed Lord's, they are concluded in three and thirty years, or whether they are prolonged to old age."[1]

Flo had administered more than one hundred nurses during the war. Six had died. The toll for the soldiers was staggering. Nearly three thousand had died in battle, but another twenty thousand died of wounds or sickness! And of the living—nurses and soldiers alike—who could say how mentally wounded they would be for the rest of their lives? It was not until July 16 that the last patient left the Barrack Hospital in Scutari. Only then could Flo herself leave. Letters from home said England waited impatiently to fete her. She wanted none of it. On the return trip, she and Aunt Mai traveled incognito. From Paris, Flo traveled alone, and upon reaching London, she took the railroad north to the family's summer home. It was a pleasant August evening when she trudged up from the rail station to Lea Hurst.

"Miss Florence!"

The housekeeper burst out of the house and ran to her. But Flo quickly claimed her privacy. She not only refused to make a public appearance but refused to attend any public ceremony. Nor would she issue a statement. Getting credit for God's work shamed her. The Nightingales respected her privacy, but Flo found no peace at Lea Hurst. Her memory of the thousands of dead soldiers prodded her. She must do something for the living soldiers, present and future. At last she endeavored to meet privately with the powers-that-be. But in the aftermath of the war, no one was anxious to discuss such matters. Lord Panmure was not available. And though Sidney Herbert met with her briefly, he made it clear he had no stomach for more fighting. He appeared very ill.

Then in September, a letter arrived.

"Sir James Clark invites me to visit him at his Birk Hall in Scotland," she told Mama and Parthe.

Mama screamed, "That's a fifteen-minute walk from Balmoral and Queen Victoria!"

Of course, that was the hidden intent behind the invitation. Staying with James Clark was a means for Flo to visit Queen Victoria and Prince Albert discreetly. She flew into action. There was much to do before she went to Scotland. She met with John McNeill, Colonel Tulloch, and Colonel Lefroy. They inundated her with facts about the army. Flo was now very enamored with statistics. This was her outlet for the fondness she had long held for the purity of mathematics. Flo and her allies formulated a very ambitious plan. Flo would solicit the queen to form a royal commission to investigate not only the medical procedures of the army but its education and administration of the common soldier. After all, Queen Victoria said that the welfare of the common soldier was one of her greatest interests.

James Clark prepared Flo for her royal audience. "The queen is quite nervous about meeting you. Almost terrified."

"I will do everything I can to put her at ease," Flo promised.

But Flo was astounded. The queen now had eight children. She had reigned for nearly twenty years. She had handled so many difficult situations. For years, Flo had heard about the queen's deftness—not only at ceremonies but at social gatherings. And Queen Victoria was almost terrified of *her?* What kind of monstrous heroine had Flo become?

On the afternoon of September 21, James Clark took Flo to Balmoral. Flo could scarcely believe she was entering the fabled ivory-hued castle. Although Prince Albert was calm, the fear in the queen's large blue eyes could easily be seen by Flo. The monarch's fair skin flushed, but within minutes, she relaxed. Flo had the ability to set others at ease. Her demure and gracious demeanor could melt just about anyone. Queen Victoria sounded almost giddy with relief as she asked for the royal children to meet Miss Nightingale. Vicky was the oldest at sixteen. Crown Prince Edward, called "Bertie," was one year younger. The children were very respectful, although the youngest seemed to blink with their eyes, "Can this frail, insignificant woman be the legendary Florence Nightingale?" After the children were dismissed, the queen initiated a conversation.

"You have no self-importance or humbug," said the queen. "No wonder the soldiers love you so."

Flo was encouraged to make her plea. For over an hour she presented her case for reform of the army. Later, at Birk Hall, Flo learned from James Clark that Queen Victoria and Prince Albert were overwhelmed by her. They marveled that she was even more magnificent than her reputation. The queen couldn't get over the fact that Flo traveled around alone, that she refused all public acclaim, and that she was so totally forgiving.

"But I'm not important at all," protested Flo. "What did the queen say about all the important things we discussed?"

"Patience, my dear Miss Nightingale," said the elderly doctor soothingly.

During her stay in Scotland, Flo saw the royals on several occasions. Years had passed since Flo had wrestled with metaphysics; now she renewed that contest with Prince Albert. He loved to talk about metaphysics. Once, she accompanied the queen and the royal family to church. But the most surprising event of all was when Queen Victoria, taking her cue from Flo, arrived one day at Birk Hall, quite alone!

"What a time in history this is for Britain," glowed the queen. "The most celebrated man in the world is our great missionary explorer David Livingstone. I can't wait to meet him when he returns from Africa. And the most celebrated woman in the world I'm talking to at this very moment."

Praise meant nothing to Flo, except perhaps that it pleased the person giving the praise or that it was a gauge of what Flo might accomplish toward her goals. Her mission these days was to help the common soldier by means of a royal commission. One man remained to be convinced. The queen could not issue a warrant for a commission to investigate the army unless the secretary of war, Lord

Panmure, advised and consented. To this end, the queen informed Flo that Lord Panmure would be at Balmoral the next week. The queen insisted that Flo give her a draft of the main issues. This she would send to Lord Panmure to digest before the meeting.

"Praise God, Lord Panmure can no longer avoid me," Flo congratulated herself later.

Lord Panmure was nicknamed the "Bison." At Flo's first encounter with him at Balmoral, on October 5, 1856, she saw why. His head was huge, crowned with unruly tufts of hair. And to make the comparison perfect, he swayed his head side to side as he talked! But never had Flo been so disappointed in a man's character. He scorned the reports of the commissions he had sent to the Crimea. If their conclusions had not been so devastating, he would have squelched them. But Flo consoled herself with the fact that ultimately he had not squelched them.

"If the facts are strong enough, the man will act," she reasoned.

After the meeting, she was told by several sources that Lord Panmure had been impressed by her. A royal commission seemed a certainty. Her confidence in success was reinforced when Lord Panmure came to see her privately at Birk Hall. Flo was asked to submit a confidential report outlining the royal commission, even recommending its eight members. She selected James Clark, Dr. Sutherland, and six others, all of whom had much to commend them. Under no circumstances could Dr. Hall, her old nemesis in the Crimea, be included.

She needed facts to back her position. In a frenzy of

activity, she compiled a report of nearly one thousand pages, with copious statistics. One fact she uncovered was shocking. Even in peacetime, young soldiers in the prime of life died at twice the rate of average citizens! How could that be, except for negligence on the army's part? Her report included a chilling line: "Our soldiers enlist to death in the barracks." Surely that would sway anyone with a good heart and an open mind!

She sent her report to Lord Panmure. It seemed the naming of a royal commission was imminent, yet weeks passed with no obvious progress. Was Lord Panmure deliberately stalling? Did he think this was just one more report to make his life miserable? Apparently to mollify her, Lord Panmure sent her blueprints of Britain's first purely military medical facility, Netley Hospital. But he underestimated Flo. She studied the plans, consulted experts, and compiled statistics from British and foreign sources, then issued her response: Netley Hospital was a disaster in the making. Lord Panmure was stunned. He brought in his architects. The building was well under construction! Alterations now would cost a fortune, he quickly informed Flo.

"Perhaps I will advise my old neighbor of this disaster," mulled Flo.

During Christmastime of 1856, Flo dined with her neighbor Lord Palmerston at Broadlands. He was kind enough to hear her complaints about Netley Hospital. He trusted her judgment and heeded her compelling arguments that the hospital was an architectural marvel but a calamity for patients. Because Lord Palmerston was also the prime minister of Great Britain, he was very upset that such a poor hospital was being built. On January 17, he notified Lord Panmure that construction on the hospital must stop. The secretary of war was stupefied. How would he explain scrapping such a large investment? He decided to expedite construction. Once the hospital was completed, even the prime minister would have to accept it. Maybe even Florence Nightingale.

With reluctance, Flo did accept Netley Hospital. But she was depressed. As champion for the common soldier, she was faring badly. Not only had she lost the battle over the hospital, but she had probably lost the war. Would Lord Panmure now retaliate for her interference by shelving the royal commission? Assurances from the secretary that the plan was still underway failed to comfort her. She no longer trusted the man. At long last, she decided to draw on her capital with the British people. She would go public, she advised Sidney Herbert, if the royal commission was not launched. Herbert, she assumed, would advise Lord Panmure of her intentions.

On April 27, 1857, Lord Panmure visited her at the Burlington Hotel in London. "Perhaps you would be so kind as to review the plans for the royal commission," he said, "that will be presented to Her Royal Majesty?"

As badly as Flo wanted the commission to convene, she did not rubber-stamp Panmure's plans. The eight members he had picked for the commission were pawns of the army. They were not acceptable. The secretary took a deep breath and changed the composition of the committee. Yes, he would include James Clark, and Dr. Sutherland, and so on. Only one army pawn remained on the commission. Flo was pleased. The only thing better would have been for her to chair the commission herself, but Britain was not ready for anything that radical. Instead, her good friend Sidney Herbert would be chairman.

"At long last the reform will begin!" she gloried.

In May, the royal commission was launched with its first meeting. Flo worked tirelessly behind the scenes. She coached witnesses and visited hospitals to gather more statistics. In awe, Dr. Sutherland told Aunt Mai, "She is one of the most gifted creatures God ever made." Flo labored the entire summer for the commission, while enduring the aggravation of Parthe and Mama in their Burlington Hotel suite. She fumed that "two people in tolerable and even perfect health lie on the sofa all day, doing absolutely nothing." A wealthy widower, Sir Harry Verney of Buckinghamshire, began calling, not hiding his interest in marrying Flo. Although he was an enlightened philanthropist, she rejected him. Mama was quick to see opportunity there for Parthe, who was now thirty-eight. Thus the two schemed to redirect Sir Harry's interest to Parthe.

Irritated by the distractions created by her mother and sister, Flo took one footman and slipped off to lodgings at Malvern, a fashionable resort area in the Midlands. The work of the royal commission was soon completed, but not yet presented in final form. Flo began a book on nursing she knew only she could write. Dr. Sutherland visited and found her near a nervous breakdown. He implored Aunt Mai to come and pamper her.

By October, Flo had recovered enough to return to the Burlington Hotel. She continued to work on her book. As the months passed, she fretted over the lack of progress of the royal commission. Her worries were borne out in February 1858, when Lord Palmerston's government fell. Would Lord Derby's new government sympathize with reform? Then her great friend Alexis Soyer, who had been enlisted to help, died. Sidney Herbert looked sicker every day, and though Flo didn't like to admit it, her own health was precarious.

"We must not relent in our pursuit of reform," she told her allies.

No one any longer thought reform would be easy. Under the Earl of Derby's new government, the old army stalwarts in the War Office sought to thwart—or at least stall—every reform, much as the medical staff in the Crimea had hampered Flo's efforts during the war. It was going to be a long battle—perhaps even a losing battle. Flo was elated, though, when Parthe married Sir Harry Verney. His Claydon House was in John Bunyan country, forty miles north of London. Flo's attitude toward the distant Parthe softened.

The only good thing about having the Earl of Derby as prime minister was the fact that his son, Lord Stanley, was secretary of state for India. Flo knew Lord Stanley well. Soon she was pushing for another royal commission, this one to reform the army in India. To those not familiar with India, this seemed a small undertaking. But the truth was that the army had an enormous presence in India, virtually running Britain's "crown jewel." In May 1859, the royal commission on India was granted, and Flo threw herself headlong into that endeavor too! In June 1859, the government fell again. Lord Palmerston returned, this time not with Lord Panmure as secretary of war, but Sidney Herbert!

"If Sidney Herbert can keep his health, our battle for reform is won," declared Flo.

Flo had proposed an Army Medical School in 1857. In 1859, it was formally initiated and due to receive its first students the next year. In the meantime, Flo's health failed even more. She became breathless. Standing made her faint. Food nauseated her. Some hinted that her illnesses were feigned to avoid visitors, even family, but wouldn't she have done that years before? Would her greatest collapse have occurred *after* Parthe had married? Whatever people thought, she labored on, now usually lying on a couch in a sea of books and notes. Dr. Sutherland served as her legs, helping constantly by gathering data. Flo kept a residence in the suburb of London called Hampstead but kept her address secret from everyone but the closest of family and friends.

In spite of her frailty, she labored incessantly, working on a dozen things at once. When one subject felt stale, she switched to another. She had recently published a 108-page book on hospitals for the public. She worked on projects to support the royal commission on Britain. She compiled statistics for the royal commission on India. She toiled on refinements in the new Army Medical School. She planned a school of nursing with the Florence Nightingale Fund, which had swollen since the end of the Crimean War. She agonized over theology and metaphysics, compiling her thoughts in hundreds of pages.

She also completed her nursing book.

FIFTEEN

Flo prefaced her book *Notes on Nursing: What It Is, and What It Is Not* with, "The following notes are by no means intended as a rule of thought by which nurses can teach themselves to nurse, still less as a manual to teach nurses to nurse. They are meant simply to give hints for thought to women who have personal charge of the health of others."[1]

Flo poured her knowledge into the book, which had chapter headings such as "Ventilation and Warming," "Petty Management," "Taking Food," "What Food?," "Bed and Bedding," "Light," "Cleanliness of Rooms and Walls," "Personal Cleanliness," "Chattering Hopes and Advice," and "Observation of the Sick." Her hundreds of anecdotes, rules, and comments were touted as "gems" by her colleagues:

> *It has been said and written scores of times, that every woman makes a good nurse. I believe, on the contrary, that the very elements of nursing are all but unknown.*
>
> *...[On the other hand], it is constantly objected, "But how can I obtain this medical knowledge? I am not a doctor. I must leave this to doctors." Oh, mothers of families! You who say this, do you know that one in every seven infants in this civilized land of England perishes before it is one year old?*
>
> *...Symptoms or the sufferings generally considered*

to be inevitable and incident to the disease are very often not symptoms of the disease at all, but of something quite different—of the want of fresh air, or of light, or of warmth, or of quiet, or of cleanliness, or of punctuality and care in the administration of diet, of each or of all of these.

. . . There are five essential points in securing the health of houses,

1. Pure air.

2. Pure water.

3. Efficient drainage.

4. Cleanliness.

5. Light.

Without these, no house can be healthy. And it will be unhealthy just in proportion as they are deficient.

. . . The very first canon of nursing, the first and the last thing upon which a nurse's attention must be fixed, the first essential to a patient, without which all the rest you can do for him is as nothing, with which I had almost said you may leave all the rest alone, is this: To keep the air he breathes as pure as the external air, without chilling him.

. . . Second only to their need of fresh air is their need of light. . . . It is a curious thing to observe how almost all patients lie with their faces turned to the light, exactly as plants always make their way towards the light; a patient will even complain that it gives him pain "lying on that side." "Then why do you lie on that side?" He does not know, but we do.

. . . Unnecessary noise, or noise that creates an

expectation in the mind, is that which hurts a patient. It is rarely the loudness of the noise. . .[but] he cannot bear the talking, still less the whispering, especially if it be of a familiar voice, outside his door. . .and [he] knows they are talking about him.

. . .Walking on tip-toe, doing any thing in the room very slowly, are injurious, for exactly the same reasons. A firm light quick step, a steady quick hand are the desiderata; not the slow, lingering, shuffling foot, the timid, uncertain touch. Slowness is not gentleness.

. . .I have seen, in fevers (and felt, when I was a fever patient myself), the most acute suffering. . .[from the patient] not being able to see out of the window, and the knots in the wood being the only view. I shall never forget the rapture of fever patients over a bunch of bright-colored flowers. . . . [Never] deny him, on the plea of unhealthiness, a glass of cut-flowers, or a growing plant.

. . .To the large majority of very weak patients it is quite impossible to take any solid food before 11:00 a.m. . . . For weak patients have generally feverish nights and, in the morning, dry mouths; and, if they could eat with those dry mouths, it would be the worse for them. A spoonful of beef-tea, of arrowroot and wine, of egg flip, every hour, will give them the requisite nourishment.

. . .Support, with the pillows, the back below the breathing apparatus, to allow the shoulders room to fall back, and to support the head, without throwing it forward. The suffering of dying patients is immensely

increased by neglect of these points. And many an invalid, too weak to drag about his pillows himself, slips his book or anything at hand behind the lower part of his back to support it.

. . .The only way to remove dust. . .is to wipe everything with a damp cloth. . . . All furniture ought to be made as that it may be wiped with a damp cloth without injury to itself.

. . .As for walls, the worst is the papered wall; the next worst is plaster. But the plaster can be redeemed by frequent lime-washing. . . . The best wall now extant is oil paint. . . . The best wall for a sickroom or ward that could be made is pure white [and] non-absorbent.

. . .The amount of relief and comfort experienced by the sick after the skin has been carefully washed and dried, is one of the commonest observations made at a sick bed.

. . .Every nurse ought to be careful to wash her hands very frequently during the day. If her face too, so much the better.

. . .Compare the dirtiness of the water in which you have washed when it is cold without soap, cold with soap, hot with soap. You will find the first has hardly removed any dirt at all, the second a little more, the third a great deal more.

. . .The most important practical lesson that can be given to nurses is to teach them what to observe—how to observe what symptoms indicate improvement— what the reverse—which are of importance—which

are of none—which are the evidence of neglect—and
of what kind of neglect. . . . All this is what ought to
make part, and an essential part, of the training of
every nurse.[2]

What had she left out of *Notes on Nursing*? It seemed nothing. Her approach was many pronged. One mandate was a sanitary environment for the patient. Another was consideration for the patient's troubled feelings. A third was for shrewd observations. Flo's book was received with acclaim. It was a masterpiece. She was far too modest, critics said. A woman could indeed learn to be a nurse just from reading her book. Thousands of copies were sold.

Her book on theology and metaphysics was far more imprecise. She titled it *Suggestions for Thought*, and it reflected her dilemma: She had no time to thoroughly synthesize the subjects. She published nearly one thousand pages of her thoughts for private distribution. She drew on her background in Unitarianism, her extensive reading and conversations with Christian Bunsen, Thomas Carlyle, Harriet Martineau, George Eliot, and many other "advanced" thinkers. She incorporated previous writings like *Cassandra* and others as far back as 1846. Her editing was halfhearted, and, in contrast to *Notes on Nursing*, *Suggestions for Thought* rambled and repeated itself, even contradicting itself. Still, powerhouse intellects like John Stuart Mill glanced through it and praised her efforts. He saw some real nuggets of original wisdom in the pages. But not one reviewer advised her to publish it. It needed strong editing.

Aunt Mai wondered whether, in trying to be rational, Flo had not forced herself into a theology that she did not really believe. In her treatise, Flo was willing to admit only that God was benevolent and His very thoughts were immutable physical laws. That made her not a Christian but a theist. Aunt Mai believed that Flo was more in harmony with the book of John, which strongly affirmed that Jesus was divine. And John was mystical, just as Flo tended to be. But how was a devotee of the book of John to take the highly critical approach to theology that characterized the times? Flo was confounded by this dilemma.

"I wanted this to develop into an aid for the common people to find God," she told Aunt Mai. "But perhaps others have done it already—and much better."

Flo sensed that she would never find the time necessary to edit the writings for general publication. Another of Flo's projects was more fruitful. She had long wanted to start a school of nursing. In her many visits to hospitals, Flo had met Mrs. Sarah Wardroper, matron of St. Thomas Hospital in London. The matron, too, had "no humbug or self-importance" and sparkled with good humor. Best of all, she sounded eminently practical, frankly admitting to Flo that a school for nursing within a hospital would be resisted by many doctors. Nevertheless, Flo knew she had discovered the woman who could start such a venture. In May 1859, she began to work out the funding for a school of nursing at St. Thomas Hospital with money from the Florence Nightingale Fund.

On June 24, 1860—just after her fortieth birthday—the "Nightingale Training School for Nurses" opened with fifteen probationers under their supervisor Mrs. Wardroper. Each woman had a private room in a new wing of St. Thomas Hospital, board, as well as a brown uniform with white cap and apron. In addition to training the probationers to nurse real patients in the wards, three senior doctors gave lectures to ground the women in the medical science of the day. Those trainees who successfully completed the one year of training were certified and registered as nurses.

"The program is revolutionary," admitted several medical professionals.

Flo monitored the school like a hawk. Her complex evaluation system for each candidate had five possible grades for twenty different attributes. Any moral failing, such as drunkenness or excessive flirting, meant immediate dismissal. Flo had a long history of enforcing morality. She had shipped several nurses back from the Crimea for failing to live up to Christian standards. Still, with Flo and Mrs. Wardroper shepherding their flock, only two of the fifteen failed to qualify at the end of the year at St. Thomas. The thirteen successful candidates were snapped up by local hospitals. Flo implored these highly qualified young nurses not to hire out to wealthy private families. They must serve everyone, not just the well-to-do.

Shortly after her school for nurses opened, in September 1860, the Army Medical School opened at long last. In spite of Queen Victoria's backing, indeed Lord Palmerston's backing too, the battle with the old army officers had been won only because Sidney Herbert had personally hammered it to a conclusion. Even as professors taught the school's first ten students, the old army bureaucracy harassed them over every requisition. In spite of the limited success, Flo had been critical of Sidney Herbert's drive and determination. She often wrote him stinging letters. Was he at fifty succumbing to her Papa's indolence? Then on December 5, 1860, he visited Flo at Hampstead.

"My dear Mr. Herbert, your face is puffy and you look extremely tired," she said, always sensitive to such things.

"I fear I have a kidney ailment," he told her.

"That is a reasonable diagnosis."

"Perhaps incurable."

"Nonsense," she retorted, doing an about-face. "Organs mend. I see no sign whatever that a kidney disease is bringing you down."

But by June of 1861, he told her the army reform was too much for him. He simply had no energy to overcome the constant haggling with the old army establishment. Like Flo, he often spent the entire day on the sofa. Flo refused to admit he was failing and urged him to continue. He declined. Were they to lose their battle for army reform after four hard-fought years? "What about our duty to the common soldier?" she railed. She angrily accused him of having a winning hand, yet quitting the game. What a humiliation! He trudged away.

On July 16, Sidney Herbert informed Flo that he had sent his resignation to Lord Palmerston. His successor was George Lewis. On August 2, at his great Wilton estate, Sidney Herbert died. Flo was devastated. She had belittled his incurable illness. Was she blinded by her own ambition? She had prodded him, needled him. Consumed by guilt, she reflected on what she and Sidney Herbert had accomplished. Of course, they had started the Army Medical School. They had the worst barracks demolished and new ones constructed. Kitchen ovens were provided to the common soldiers. Good nutrition was pushed through training schools for cooks. Reading rooms were provided at many bases now. So were recreational facilities. Mortality had dropped markedly where they had been allowed to make improvements. But the improvements were not universal. And so much remained to be done.

"Frankly, with Sidney Herbert's death, the reform of the British army is over," groaned Flo. "We just wanted to allow the soldiers to be men and not condemn them to be brutal beasts."

Although her goals were frustrated, Flo's relations with her family were excellent now. Her relationship with Parthe's husband, Sir Harry Verney, was warm. At the end of 1861, he helped her move to one of his residences on South Street in London. But December 1861 brought another obstacle to Flo's goals. Prince Albert, only forty-two years old, had died of typhoid fever. Queen Victoria was paralyzed with grief.

SIXTEEN

Flo became even more depressed. Aunt Mai was no longer with her. Hilary had lived with her for a year but was forced to rejoin her family. Flo could not read a newspaper—she could not bear to see the names of those recently lost to her—but she still wrote letters. She wrote to Mama on March 7, 1862:

> It takes a deal of faith to make God's will mine. For indeed I don't see how in any world there could be such a combination for good as that which existed between me and my lost ones—here. . . . I think what I have felt most (during my last three months of extreme weakness) is the not having one single person to give me one inspiring word or even one correct fact. I am glad to end a day which can never come back. . . . The Queen, poor thing, is more bowed to the earth (her own expression) than ever. . . . Lord Palmerston says she is half the size she was. . . . People say that time heals the deepest griefs. It is not true.[1]

Reform was at a standstill—or it seemed that way, because for several years, she had advanced a dozen projects at once. Her Training School for Nurses still operated smoothly, but with Sidney Herbert gone, none of her friends had real influence with the War Office. Flo was still much in demand as a source for information though. She knew the histories of the various departments in the War Office. She knew about hundreds of transactions. She knew where documents could be found. She even had copies of some documents that the War Office had lost! Ministers, clerks, and secretaries deluged her with requests for information.

"I can't complain that I'm not busy," she told herself.

Reform for India had stalled too. Flo saw that it would be a very long struggle with but tiny victories. She fought poor health and depression, and she became very difficult. When the queen of Holland wanted to see her, Flo refused. Only Clarkey, the Verneys, and the Nightingales could assume she would receive them. Then, in the summer of 1865, she refused to see even Clarkey.

"It is quite, quite, quite impossible. . . ," read her note to Clarkey, who sat in Flo's downstairs foyer![2]

Only later did Flo realize how rude she had been to her dear old friend. Was she going mad? Friends tried to placate her—by letter. She admitted to some—by letter— that, as poor as her physical health was, her mental health was worse. Flo was in no way prepared for the news that Hilary had cancer. She had fallen out with Hilary, who had never escaped her domestic prison. After Hilary's death, Flo suppressed her guilt with anger, writing Clarkey that the Carter family was guilty of the "most monstrous of slow murders."[3]

Few helped her more than Dr. Sutherland, a man whom she had to see because of their work. Yet he had become her "pet aversion."[4] He was going deaf and his constant "Pardon me, Miss Nightingale?" drove Flo into a rage. She no longer spoke to him. She scribbled exasperated notes like "My dear soul! It's rather late for this," and "You said you were going to lay it before your committee, you had better lay it before me!"[5] She couldn't imagine why he had taken a house farther out of London. Now she couldn't summon him on a moment's notice.

When Papa purchased the 10 South Street house for Flo, it quickly became her very own home, characterized by its brightness and lack of frills. She did, however, grace some walls with prints of Michelangelo's frescoes in the Sistine Chapel, and her household included her lady's maid, five housemaids, a cook, and a handyman.

Flo still loved to read and take notes. Besides reading medical journals, she corresponded with doctors. The news in medicine these days was very exciting. Chemist Louis Pasteur of France was trying to prove that tiny organisms, or "germs," caused disease. Joseph Lister, a Yorkshire man who doctored in Scotland, was experimenting with the carbolic acid used to disinfect sewers. He applied carbolic acid to his surgical instruments before surgery and to the open wound after surgery. Flo heard that his first results were very encouraging.

She read belated accounts of the Crimean War. Many were self-serving. Few were masterpieces. Ironically the truest was by a Russian artillery officer, Leo Tolstoy, who commanded a cannon battery in the Fourth Bastion, the most forward Russian position during the fall of Sebastopol. His writing of actual combat made other accounts of the war appear to be childish scribbles.

She had no lack of correspondence, no lack of people seeking advice on many topics. She monitored her nursing school and advised those who wanted to start others. She wrote hundreds of letters to her staff and the nurses they had certified. She lauded Agnes Jones's monumental effort in the Liverpool Workhouse Infirmary. But hard-focused projects were a thing of the past for Flo. She tried at one point to resurrect her *Suggestions for Thought* but once again abandoned it. The book of John triumphed over modern rationalism.

"The mystical faith illuminated in St. John's Gospel, however incompletely I have lived it, was and is enough for me," she at last admitted in a letter.

She was very worn out for her age. And her family and friends were dying. In 1874, Papa died at eighty, which necessitated the vacating of Embley Park so that Shore Smith could at long last inherit it. Mama died in 1880 at ninety-two; Clarkey in 1883 at eighty-six; Richard Monckton Milnes in 1885 at seventy-six; Aunt Mai in 1889 at ninety; Parthe in 1890 at seventy-one; Dr. Sutherland in 1891 at eighty-three; Aunt Julia in 1893 at eighty-four. Sir Harry Verney died in 1894 at ninety-three. Flo's "boy Shore" died that year too, at a mere sixty years of age.

So many had died!

Flo saw the new century in. So did Queen Victoria, who by now had reigned for more than sixty years! Flo herself had passed into legend as "the lady with the lamp." Even the American Henry Wadsworth Longfellow romanticized her in his poem "Santa Filomena":

Lo! in that hour of misery
A lady with a lamp I see

Pass through the glimmering gloom,
And flit from room to room.
And slow, as in a dream of bliss
The speechless sufferer turns to kiss
Her shadow, as it falls
Upon the darkening walls.

Some hailed Flo as one of the three greatest figures of nineteenth-century medicine in Britain, along with James Simpson and Joseph Lister. Simpson had pioneered chloroform as an anesthetic. Lister had pioneered carbolic acid as an antiseptic. The contributions of these three had drastically reduced mortality in the sick. But praise meant little to Flo. She was ever restless. Oh, if only she could have done more. There was so much to do. Was it any wonder she was irritable? Could anyone know the frustration she felt when reform stalled? For that matter, could anyone know the frustration she had endured in the earlier years?

"Read *Cassandra,*" she muttered, "then read about Scutari."

She had gained weight with age. She appeared the stolid matron, instead of a wiry Joan of Arc. People were still in awe of her. There was little said about her that she didn't eventually hear from her hundreds of correspondents. From a gallery in 1883, Flo had watched a ceremony conducted by Queen Victoria. Later the queen was heard to gasp, "To think Florence Nightingale came to see me!"

But by 1906, the queen had died and no one requested any advice from Flo. At eighty-six, her health had failed almost completely. A visitor was never received until her caretaker had coached her first as to the caller's identity and purpose. Flo was very concerned about final arrangements too. There must be no elaborate burial in some honored place like Westminster Abbey. Besides, nothing could honor her more than common soldiers bearing her coffin to her grave next to Mama and Papa in the St. Margaret church cemetery at Wellow. She gave specific instructions as to what her epitaph must read. With that, she was satisfied to await the end.

On August 13, 1910, at the ripe old age of ninety, Florence Nightingale fell asleep and passed on into Paradise. The small cross above her grave was inscribed:

F. N.

BORN 1820

DIED 1910

FOR FURTHER READING

I. Excellent biographies:

Huxley, Elspeth. *Florence Nightingale.* New York: Putnam, 1975.

O'Malley, I. B. *Florence Nightingale, 1820–1856.* London: Thornton Butterworth, 1931.

Woodham-Smith, Cecil. *Florence Nightingale: 1820–1910.* New York: McGraw-Hill, 1951.

II. Various collections of Florence Nightingale's many writings:

Calabria, Michael D., ed. *Florence Nightingale in Egypt and Greece: Her Diary and "Visions."* Albany: State University of New York Press, 1997.

Nightingale, Florence. *Notes on Nursing: What It Is, and What It Is Not.* Cutochogue, NY: Buccaneer Books, 1976 (reprint of 1860 classic).

Poovey, Mary, ed. *Cassandra and Other Selections from Suggestions for Thought.* New York: New York University Press, 1992.

Vicinus, Martha, and Bea Nergaard, eds. *Ever Yours, Florence Nightingale: Selected Letters.* Cambridge, MA: Harvard University Press, 1990.

III. Other relevant readings:

Barbary, James. *The Crimean War*. New York: Hawthorn Books, 1970.

Longford, Elizabeth. *Queen Victoria: Born to Succeed*. New York: Harper & Row, 1964.

NOTES

CHAPTER 1
   1. I. B. O'Malley, *Florence Nightingale, 1820–1856* (London: Thornton Butterworth, 1931), 17.

CHAPTER 2
   1. Martha Vicinus and Bea Nergaard, eds., *Ever Yours, Florence Nightingale: Selected Letters* (Cambridge, MA: Harvard University Press, 1990), 14. Used with permission.
   2. O'Malley, 23.
   3. Vicinus, 14.
   4. O'Malley, 25–26.

CHAPTER 3
   1. Cecil Woodham-Smith, *Florence Nightingale, 1820–1910* (New York: McGraw-Hill, 1951), 7–8.
   2. Vicinus, 15.

CHAPTER 4
   1. O'Malley, 35.
   2. Ibid., 36.

Chapter 5

1. O'Malley, 40.
2. Woodham-Smith, 12.
3. O'Malley, 50.
4. Ibid., 50–51.

Chapter 6

1. O'Malley, 71.
2. Ibid., 69.
3. Woodham-Smith, 26.
4. Vicinus, 16.

Chapter 7

1. Vicinus, 20.
2. O'Malley, 88.
3. Ibid., 91.
4. Woodham-Smith, 34.
5. Ibid.
6. O'Malley, 94.
7. Ibid., 94–95.
8. Ibid., 97.
9. Ibid.
10. Ibid., 100.
11. Woodham-Smith, 31.
12. Ibid.
13. O'Malley, 101.
14. Ibid., 103.
15. Ibid., 104.

16. Ibid.
17. Ibid.

CHAPTER 8

1. O'Malley, 106.
2. Ibid., 107.
3. Ibid., 108.
4. Ibid., 109.
5. Ibid., 116.
6. Ibid.
7. Michael D. Calabria, *Florence Nightingale in Egypt and Greece: Her Diary and "Visions"* (Albany: State University of New York Press, 1997), 3–4. Used with permission.
8. O'Malley, 119.
9. Ibid., 120.
10. Ibid., 122.
11. Ibid., 125.
12. Ibid., 126.
13. Ibid., 127.
14. Ibid., 128.
15. Ibid.
16. Ibid., 130.

CHAPTER 9

1. Mary Keele, ed., *Florence Nightingale's Letters from Rome, 1847–8.* (Philadelphia: American Philosophical Society, 1981), 28. Used with

permission.

2. Keele, 108–113.

3. Ibid., 73.

4. O'Malley, 142.

5. Ibid., 144–145.

6. Ibid., 149.

7. Ibid., 150.

8. Anthony Sattin, ed., *Florence Nightingale's "Letters from Egypt," 1849–50.* (New York: Weidenfeld & Nicolson, 1987), 21.

9. Sattin, 26.

10. Ibid., 39.

11. Ibid., 49.

12. Ibid., 67.

13. Ibid., 81.

CHAPTER 10

1. Sattin, 85.

2. Ibid., 63

3. Calabria, 20–48.

4. Ibid., Vicinus, 41, Woodham-Smith, 53.

5. Woodham-Smith, 53.

6. Ibid.

7. Vicinus, 41–42.

8. Calabria, 55.

9. Ibid.

10. Vicinus, 44.

11. Ibid., 45–46.

12. Ibid.

13. Vicinus, 47.
14. Ibid., 57.
15. Raymond G. Herbert, *Florence Nightingale: Saint, Reformer or Rebel?* (Malabar, Florida: Robert E. Krieger Publishing, 1981), 34–52. Used with permission.

CHAPTER 11
1. Woodham-Smith, 73.
2. Vicinus, 74.
3. Woodham-Smith, 85.
4. Ibid., 86.
5. Ibid., 87–88.
6. Ibid., 91.
7. Vicinus, 83.

CHAPTER 12
1. Vicinus, 83–84.
2. Ibid.
3. Elspeth Huxley, *Florence Nightingale* (New York: Putnam, 1975), 81.
4. Vicinus, 92.
5. Ibid., 98.
6. Ibid., 109.
7. Ibid., 107.
8. Ibid.

CHAPTER 13

1. Vicinus, 114.
2. Ibid.
3. Ibid.
4. Vicinus, 116.
5. Woodham-Smith, 151.
6. Ibid.
7. Ibid.
8. Woodham-Smith, 164.
9. Vicinus, 148–149.
10. Woodham-Smith, 174.

CHAPTER 14

1. Vicinus, 157.

CHAPTER 15

1. Florence Nightingale, *Notes on Nursing: What It Is, and What It Is Not.* Reprinted by Cutochogue, (New York: Buccaneer Books, 1976), 105.
2. Ibid.

CHAPTER 16

1. Vicinus, 236–238.
2. Ibid., 262.
3. Ibid., 265.
4. Woodham-Smith, 285.
5. Ibid., 286.

Bold. Fearless. Adventurous.
Women of Courage.

Sojourner Truth
Available now
Paperback / 978-1-64352-272-2 / $9.99

Mother Teresa
Coming August 2020
Paperback / 978-1-64352-508-2 / $9.99

Corrie ten Boom
Coming December 2020
Paperback / 978-1-64352-671-3 / $9.99

This series of easy-read biographies celebrates women who lived lives committed to changing the world for better. What set them apart? The willingness to live courageously for Christ, even in the midst of impossible situations. Get inspired by their stories, celebrate their legacy, and learn that God can use each of us for mighty things. . .if we have *courage.*